Christ in Us

Christ in Us

The Exalted Christ and the Indwelling of the Holy Spirit

by

Rev. Paul A. Hughes, M.Div

God's Trombone

Library of Congress Cataloguing in Publication Data
Hughes, Paul A., 1957–
Christ in Us: The Exalted Christ and the Indwelling of the Holy Spirit.
Incorporates the content of previously copyrighted booklet *Christ within
You! The Indwelling of the Holy Spirit*, Copyright ©1993 by Paul A.
Hughes.
Includes footnotes, appendices, and index.
ISBN 978-0-6151-3840-4

ON THE COVER: "The Pentecost" by El Greco, circa 1600. Public domain, as established under U. S. law in Bridgeman v. Corel, 36 F. Supp. 2d 191 (S.D.N.Y. 1999), supported by the U. S. Supreme Court in Feist v. Rural, 499 U.S. 340 (1991)[1], applying Article I of the Constitution and the Copyright Act of 1976. Copyright claims to public domain works risk the criminal provisions of Section 506 of the Copyright Act for fraudulent use of a copyright notice.

Contents

List of Figures

List of Tables

To my maternal grandfather,
Thomas Josiah Kinard I
(1889-1971),
farmer, soldier, refinery worker,
pastor, and church planter;
and my grandmother,
Cecyle Lesley Hutchins Kinard
(1906-1988),
working beside him to the end—
true Pentecostal pioneers.

The author's writings appear regularly in the following e-mail groups:

http://groups.yahoo.com/group/biblicalspirituality/
http://groups.yahoo.com/group/Pentecostl_Theol_Soc/
http://groups.yahoo.com/group/Divine_Parody/
http://groups.yahoo.com/group/End-Time_Info/
http://groups.yahoo.com/group/manifestations/
http://groups.yahoo.com/group/Start_a_Church/
http://groups.yahoo.com/group/independent_christian_music/
http://groups.yahoo.com/group/Liberalism_Unmasked/

Music CD recordings by the author:

"Look Again" (2003)
"Christian Jazz Christmas" (2004)
"Sow in Tears, Reap in Joy" (2006)

For more information on the above, contact the author at
hugh.paul@yahoo.com

Preface

The Pentecostal Movement began at a semi-formal Bible school in Topeka, Kansas, in 1901. Reports of speaking in "unknown tongues" caused a sensation in local papers. The leader of the school, Charles Parham, carried the Pentecostal message to Houston, and William Seymour, a black man, carried it to Los Angeles. Some observers emphasized reports of emotional and theological extremes.

Extremes there were, but one would be wrong to presume emotionalism to be the basis for the Movement; for the search for Holy Spirit Baptism, of which "tongues" was one manifestation, was grounded in the experience of the Early Church described in the Bible. Jesus promised that the gift of the Holy Spirit, who would be their Teacher, would be like springs of water flowing up from within their souls, giving them power to preach and overcome opposition. Christ, exalted to the right hand of the throne of God and granted all the Father's authority, now dispenses spiritual gifts to his Church, gifts meant to mature, fortify, and empower all believers.

This volume consists of a collection of essays, research papers, articles, and other writings on the Exaltation of Christ and the Holy Spirit written over the course of more than a decade. The study of the Holy Spirit, technically called *pneumatology*, became my special area of interest after I first received the Baptism in the Holy Spirit around 1982 and began to have my first tentative experiences with manifestations of the Spirit. I had previously begun reading and studying the entire Bible, accomplished over a span of two years, and both my life and my worldview were changing drastically.

I began formal academic research of the subject while attending Southwestern Assemblies of God College and the Assemblies of God Theological Seminary. Further research lead to a deeper understanding of *christology*, particularly the Exaltation of Christ, namely, his position as administrator of Holy Spirit Baptism and the manifestations of the Spirit. Many of the research papers contained herein originate from those studies, having chosen related subjects for exegesis projects and other course assignments. Several research papers, articles, and related book reviews were published in *Paraclete*, the former theological journal of the Assemblies of God.

I continued research and writing on my own in the late 1980s and early 1990s, culminating in the practical booklet, *Christ Within You! The Indwelling of the Holy Spirit*, the chapters of which have been incorporated into this larger work. Upon reviewing this booklet, Pentecostal scholar emeritus Stanley Horton pointed out one erroneous Scripture citation, since corrected, then concluded that "on the whole, it is excellent." During the same period, I was a frequent contributor to the sermon column of a local newspaper, the *Polk County Enterprise* of Livingston, Texas, in which several additional articles were originally published.

I maintain the firm conviction is that the gifts of the Holy Spirit, intended for the operation of the Church during this present Church Age, have been and continue to be neglected even by so-called Full Gospel believers. Reasons for this neglect include an often paranoid fear of fanaticism; the lack of respectability accorded to manifestations in society, especially speaking in tongues; and the simple fact that it is easier to resort to manmade traditions, institutions, and methods than to rely on the Holy Spirit. Working in the realm of the Holy Spirit requires an extent of sacrifice of one's carnal thinking and self-interest that most Christians are unwilling to make.

I sincerely hope that this volume will serve to emphasize the need for the Baptism and gifts of the Holy Spirit in the Church and in the world today. Further, I pray that these pages may assuage the fears of those who do not understand the subject, stem the prejudices of those who were taught to consider manifestations of the Spirit to be low-class or "of the devil," and most of all encourage the reader to follow the advice of an earlier and greater Paul to "covet earnestly the best gifts," especially those which "excel to the edifying of the church" (1 Corinthians 12:31, 14:12).

Rev. Paul A. Hughes
Liberty, Texas
December 2006

Chapter 1.   It Don't Matter, If It Ain't Spiritual!

Consider:

All the high-toned prayers,
All the times of weeping before the Lord,
All the days spent fasting for whatever reason,
And all the gallons of tears expended—
It don't matter, if it ain't spiritual.

And all the services attended,
All the hours of Bible study,
All the coins dropped in the offering plate,
And even paying every last cent of tithe—
It don't matter, if it ain't spiritual.

And all the fine musical performances,
All the songs you've written,
All the books you've published,
All the classes you've taught, and sermons preached—
It don't matter, if it ain't spiritual.

We do so many things in the flesh,
Things that look impressive and sound good,
If we listen to ourselves, our friends, and the world,
We will think that because we're busy working,
We're getting the job done.

You might be mad at me for saying so,
But check me out if this isn't 100 percent Biblical:
God once commanded the sacrifice of bulls and goats,
But the bulls and goats didn't matter;
He wanted men to honor him with their lips,
But if their hearts were far from him, the words didn't matter;
Christ sent spiritual gifts for our benefit,
But unless they were done in love, they didn't matter;
And Paul even said that some church services
Did more harm than good.

God called us to be spiritual people,
He seeks those who will worship him in Spirit and in Truth,
To live according to the Spirit and not the flesh,
To sacrifice the honors and pleasures of this world
With our eyes set on the goal of the next.
So next time you aim to do something for God, remember:
It don't matter, if it ain't spiritual!

Chapter 2.   Christ, God's Greatest Gift*

At Christmastime, people who do not regularly attend church show up for Christmas programs, those who seldom pray recite elaborate blessings over family dinners, and people who are at best nominal Christians pay homage to God for the birth of Jesus Christ.

John 3:16 begins, "God so loved the world that He gave his only-begotten Son . . . ." It is true that the birth of Christ was a great expression of God's love for his creation. Unfortunately, most public rhetoric reduces the meaning of Christmas to "God showing He loves us by giving us a present."

However, the coming of Christ goes far beyond his simply being born. Christ's birth was just the beginning of his great work. God was giving much more than a child, but no less than the Savior of the world for all ages. John 3:16 goes on to say, ". . . that whoever believes in him might not perish, but might have eternal life."

Christ Showed Us the Way to Salvation

True service to God is not in following arbitrary rules and regulations but in loving God with all your heart, soul, and might, and loving your neighbor like yourself (Mark 12:29-31). You are required to "sell out" completely to God (Mark 10:21, Luke 12:33) and "deny yourself" (Matthew 16:24), but in doing so you inherit the "free gift" of eternal salvation (Romans 4:16, Ephesians 2:8).

Christ Paid for Our Sins for All Time

While the sacrifices of Moses' Law had to be made over and over, Christ's sacrifice on the cross was "once for all" (Hebrews 10:10-13). Christ is willing to bear the sins of anyone who will simply believe in him and entrust their sins to his great sacrifice (Hebrews 9:28).

---

* Originally Published in the *Polk County Enterprise*.

Christ Ascended to God's Right Hand

When He left the earth, Christ received his just reward for his perfect obedience to God's plan: He ascended to God's throne and took his seat at God's right hand. As God's literal "right-hand man," Christ has been granted all the power of God in order to serve and empower his Church (John 3:35, Ephesians 1:22).

Christ Continues to Save and Grant Gifts to His Church

Christ is "head" to his "body," the Church. Those who enter into his Church become a part of him, figuratively and spiritually. As part of Christ, Christians are nourished and cared for as parts of his body (Ephesians 4:15-16). Those who are "in Christ" remain covered by the blood of his sacrifice and enter into eternal salvation with him (Romans 8:1-3).

More than that, Christ wields all the power of God in behalf of his Church. He dispenses spiritual gifts through the Holy Spirit to aid the operation of the Church (1 Corinthians 14:2-5) and to enable Christians to preach the gospel with divine power (1 Corinthians 2:4-5, 1 Thessalonians 1:5). By extension, those who are "gifted" for leadership are also considered gifts to the Church (1 Corinthians 12:28, Ephesians 4:11-12). Thus Jesus Christ rules and reigns over his Church from his seat in God's throne.

God's gift of Christ was much more than simply showing us He loves us by sending a baby to be born. God sent his one and only Son to live, die, triumph over sin, and reign over us. Jesus Christ was more than just a good man, a moral teacher, a well-meaning man who tried to save the world but lost his own life.

Christ was the one for whom this world was made in the first place (Colossians 1:16-19). The world as a whole has not yet been forcibly put under his rule (Hebrews 2:8). In this Age of Grace, Christ does not force submission on us. But ultimately, in God's time, all things will be put in subjection to Christ (1 Corinthians 15:28, Revelation 19:15).

This Christmas, celebrate Christ as more than just a child in a manger. Celebrate him for all that He is: Savior, Lord of the Church, ultimate Lord of the earth. If you let him, He can be your personal Savior and Lord, as well, and the greatest friend you will ever find.

Chapter 3.   The Holy Spirit Still Works*

Most people are used to hearing the phrase, "Father, Son, and Holy Spirit" (or "Ghost") at funerals, baptisms, and other church-related events. Some may even grasp the concept of the Trinity or Godhead, the "Three in One." But few grasp the nature, role, and significance of the Holy Spirit in the world today.

Even many who are Christians are like the believers at Ephesus who, when asked, "Have you received the Holy Spirit since you believed?" answered, "We have not so much as heard whether there is any Holy Spirit" (Acts 19:2). So let us all remain like the Jews at Berea, who "received the Word with all readiness of mind, and searched the Scriptures daily, whether those things were so" (Acts 17:11).

First of all, the Holy Spirit is a *person*, not an impersonal force or another word for God. The Holy Spirit was present and active in Creation (Genesis 1:2). The Spirit, like any other person, can be vexed or grieved (Isaiah 63:10, Ephesians 4:30). He can speak, as He did through David (2 Samuel 23:2). The Spirit is "another Paraclete" *like* Jesus (but not the same person as Jesus), sent in Jesus' place to be Teacher, Ambassador, Judge, Helper, and Comforter to the Church (John chapters 14-16).

The Holy Spirit is the instrument by whom God the Father works: thus He wields all the power of God. (I have already mentioned Creation.) In Moses' time, the Spirit imparted special knowledge and skill to the builders of the Tabernacle and the Ark of the Covenant, enabling the craftsmen to construct them with high artistry according to God's specifications (Exodus 31).

The Spirit worked in and through all the prophets, granting to them the words of God and enabling them to work great miracles. To Ezekiel, the Spirit was "the hand of the Lord," which transported him by visions to view faraway places and future events (Ezekiel 3:14, 22, 24). The prophet Micah wrote, "I am full of power by the Spirit of the Lord, and of judgment, and of might, to declare unto Jacob his transgression, and to Israel his sin" (Micah 3:8).

After the death and Resurrection of Jesus Christ, however, a fundamental change took place. The fundamental nature and purpose of the Spirit did not

* Originally Published in the *Polk County Enterprise*, April 21 and 28, 1991.

change, but the breadth of his outpouring did. Jesus had promised his disciples that they would receive power from the Holy Spirit to be his witnesses with miraculous signs (Luke 24:49, Acts 1:8, etc.). The risen Christ ascended to the right hand of God, where He now reigns over all things and dispenses gifts to mankind by the Holy Spirit (Romans 8:34; Ephesians 1:19-23, 4:7-16; Colossians 1:15-19).

The fundamental change was this: before, the Spirit of God was only poured out upon prophets, priests, and kings. In other words, only a few were privileged to be used by the Spirit. In the Church Age, however, the Spirit would be poured out upon "all flesh" (Acts 2:16-18). This includes both young and old, male and female, mighty and lowly. In fact, the outpouring of the Holy Spirit is available even today for all who believe in Jesus Christ!

We still live in the Church Age. It was begun by Jesus, and will be concluded in power by Jesus when He returns (1 Thessalonians 4:13-18).

Sometimes Christians feel like they have been left in the lurch, being required to achieve perfection beyond human strength, fight battles against overwhelming odds, and fulfill impossible demands. That is what it is like, trying to serve God in human strength alone. Why should you keep trying and failing in your human strength when you can triumph in Jesus Christ through the power of the Holy Spirit?

The Spirit provides a "power assist," sort of like power steering in your car, which multiplies your efforts. God only asks that you do what you can do. If you are walking in the Spirit in obedience to God's will, He will do the rest, and get the job done.

But only to the extent that you lend yourself in obedience to God and the power of the Holy Spirit can you expect him to work through you. You never really "have" the Spirit—you must let *him* have *you*.

According to the Bible, the Spirit is the key to God's provision in our lives (John 15:4-7, 16:13-15) and to overcoming sin (Galatians 5:16, Ephesians 6:12). He gives us assurance that we are children of God (Romans 8:15-16, Galatians 5:16). He helps us get our prayers answered, since we do not know what to ask for (Romans 8:26, 1 Corinthians 2:9-16)—though we cannot expect God to answer prayers that are out of his will (James 4:3). The Holy Spirit is the spiritual link between us and Jesus (John 15:26, 16:13-15; 1 Corinthians 12:3).

Through the Spirit, Jesus bestows miraculous gifts to us in order to minister to others (Romans 12:3-8, 1 Corinthians 12-14, Ephesians 4:11-16). As we allow his gifts to work through us and in us, we begin to bring forth "good fruit." The fruit that is from the Spirit includes *love, joy, peace, patience, gentleness, kindness, faithfulness, humility*, and *self-control* (Galatians 5:22-23).

There are those who teach that the manifestations of the Holy Spirit passed away with the Apostles.[1] But this view has no sound basis in Scripture. Jesus promised "another Paraclete" who would "abide with you forever," "teach you all things," "reprove the world of sin," and "guide you into all truth" (John 14:16, 26; 16:8, 13). These functions of the Spirit have not ceased.

Spiritual gifts were to be for power for worldwide evangelism (Mark 16:15-18, etc.). Evangelism is the task for the entire Church Age, and is far from accomplished.

Peter's first sermon strongly implies that Spirit Baptism and manifestations would continue to be available as long as salvation by faith is preached (Acts 2:16-21, 38-39). We see spiritual gifts available on a continuing basis throughout the Book of Acts.

Paul gives practical advice on the use of tongues and other gifts in the worship of the church in 1 Corinthians 12-14. He does *not* say that love is a better gift than all others, thus rendering the rest unnecessary. (Love is after all a *fruit* of the Spirit, not a *gift*.) What he says is that any gift that is not practiced *with* godly love is of little or no worth. But such gifts, in love, shall remain necessary for edifying the Church until "that which is perfect [Jesus Christ] is come," whom we shall then "see face to face" (13:10, 12). In the meantime, if there are no *gifts* of the Spirit, there can be no *fruit* of the Spirit.

Many of the lists of spiritual gifts, like 1 Corinthians 12:28-30, mix manifestations such as miracles, healing, and tongues together with *gifted people*, including pastors, teachers, and evangelists.[2] This mix of terminology strongly implies that both spiritual gifts and commissions of leadership originate from the same source and work in similar fashion. Furthermore, without the spiritual gifts, the Church can have no spiritually gifted leaders.

---

[1] See the chapter, "Are the Anti-Pentecostal Arguments Valid?" below.
[2] See the table, "Comparison of Spiritual Gift Lists," in the Appendices.

Of course, no manifestation of the Spirit is a "new revelation" which adds to or circumvents the Bible. A genuine manifestation of the Spirit rather *confirms* Scripture, exhorting and edifying, and sometimes gives practical guidance (see Acts 9:11, 11:28, 13:2).

So how does one get this Holy Spirit? First, you must believe in Jesus and accept him as your Savior and Lord (John 3:16). Then you must open yourself up totally to the will of the Spirit, holding nothing back. That done, you will receive the Holy Spirit, for God is eager to give the Spirit to those who ask him (Luke 11:13). The gift of the Spirit is the essence of Christ's spiritual kingdom.

Granted, this "opening up" might take a little time and effort. You might have a lot of excess emotional baggage and self-will. Turn it all over to Jesus—your hurt, guilt, regrets, dreams, desires. Empty yourself, so He can fill you up.

How do you know that you have been filled (or "baptized") with the Holy Spirit? In the Bible, the most frequently mentioned evidence is speaking praises to God in languages one has never learned (*i.e.*, "tongues"). It happened at Pentecost (Acts 2:4), at the house of Cornelius (Acts 10:5-6), at Ephesus (Acts 19:6), and is implied elsewhere.

But more than that, the Spirit-filled believer can expect a new power in prayer, for Christian service, and for evangelism. He or she can expect to begin bearing fruit of the Spirit, including the holy love of 1 Corinthians 13.

Jesus did not leave us comfortless. God did not leave us powerless. He has provided spiritual power through the person and work of the Holy Spirit.

Chapter 4.   How Did Man Change When Adam Fell?*

On the sixth day of Creation, God created man. When He had created both man and woman, had given them dominion over all the animals and provided all plant life to be their food, "God saw every thing that he had made, and, behold, it was very good" (Genesis 1:31).

If this wording is significant, then "it was very good" implies that God created man perfect—without any fault, weakness, or evil tendency. God, who is all-powerful, omnipresent, and all knowing, is also of perfect intelligence and ability, and utterly holy in thought and intention. Then how could his Creation, generated from the very nature of his being, be anything less than perfect?

Still, Adam fell. How could this perfect creature, possessed with great intelligence and a yet unduplicated knowledge of God and intimacy of relationship with Him, act in willful and deliberate disobedience to Him? Was he, as has been conjectured, unaware of the magnitude of his crime and its effect upon the future of his race?[1] (But a sin of ignorance would have been forgiven.) Or was his sin due to some inherent fault or oversight on the part of his Creator? If man was thereafter in need of redemption—as he is now—in what way did man, in falling from grace, change?

Two theologians have shaped the theology of the Fall of Man more profoundly than any others. John Calvin (1509-1564) upheld the sovereignty of God in an absolute foreknowledge of future events. Man's actions, likewise, were absolutely predestined. Jacobus Arminius (1560-1609), however, while maintaining God's foreknowledge, nevertheless emphasized man's free will. The opinions of these distinguished theological rivals, along with other influential scholars, will be considered in this discussion.

Adam's Initial State

In the Genesis account, the creation of man is said to have taken place on the sixth day (or "day-age")[2] of Creation—which, along with God's formal bestowal upon man of authoritative (or intellectual) dominion over the ani-

---

* Originally published in *Paraclete* 23 (Fall 1989):20-23.

mal kingdom, was the crowning glory of God's handiwork. Since God, as if in formal celebration, "rested" on the seventh day, it would seem that man represented the completion, even the acme, of his Creation. And since God placed all the earth under man, one might assume that man was created both spiritually and functionally superior to all other terrestrial beings.

God created man, says Scripture, in his image (Genesis 1:26). It is generally agreed among scholars that this does not refer to man's physical endowments, for God is not physical, but spiritual (see John 4:24).

Calvin discusses this in his commentary on Genesis: Aristotle pictured an intellectual man ("three faculties of the soul . . . the intellect, the memory, and the will"); Augustine had speculated on a spiritual trinity in man corresponding, perhaps in *type*, to the Trinity. Still, Calvin goes on to suggest a *moral* likeness in which "perfect intelligence flourished and reigned, uprightness attended as its companion, and all the senses were prepared and molded for due obedience to reason."[3]

That man was created in God's image implies an ideal initial moral state. Calvin upholds this ideal state of Adam.[4] On the other hand, Jonathan Edwards—an 18th-century American Puritan in many ways "more Calvinistic" than Calvin—considered that from the beginning, man had an "internal fixed propensity" to sin.[5] Man's tendency is to "sin immediately, as soon as [he is] capable of it, and to sin continually and progressively."[6] Man is inherently evil, and it was only a matter of time before Adam sinned. In this initial state, however, Adam was able to stand in the presence of God (Genesis 2:19; 3:8f.), evidently without need of justification. The very fact that he had not yet eaten of the Tree of the Knowledge of Good and Evil implies his innocent nature. Unaware of the difference between good and evil, he literally did not know *how* to sin!

The Question of the Will

Herein lies the paradox. Adam sinned; but how could he, were he perfect? It must come down to a question of free will. Would God be glorified had He created a race of robots, creatures who worshipped and served Him, without interruption or error, by design and by necessity? Certainly not, for as one can see in this present world, true worship takes place when willful and self-concerned man, in an act of recognition of God's total sovereignty and his own utter dependence on God—as well as his great inferiority and unholiness before Him—subordinates his human will to the Divine. Even the angels were given a free will, to obey God or to rebel with Satan. Man was created with such a free will and given but one area in which to make a choice: the Tree of the Knowledge of Good and Evil.

Did God, when He created Adam, know he would make the wrong choice? Martin Luther's literary colleague, Philip Melanchthon, considered that God would in no way tempt man.[7] Calvin, on the other hand, went so far as to say that the Fall was engineered by God "in order that [man] might perceive the life of man without God to be wretched and lost, and therefore differing nothing from death."[8] Edwards would support the idea of a predetermined Fall, saying that God knows with certainty what any individual will do in any given situation, at any given time.[9] The Fall, then, was planned ahead of time, and God knew that man would fall.

Arminius would beg to differ. He saw man as a free moral agent with "freedom from the control or jurisdiction of one who commands, and from an obligation to render obedience," and "from necessity, whether this proceeds from an external cause compelling, or from a nature inwardly determining absolutely to one thing."[10] By his formulation, Adam could have continued forever in innocence, had he continually chosen to obey. Then the Fall must have been an act of willful disobedience, not necessarily due to an inherent fault or a predetermined Fall. This view agrees most readily with the tenor of Scripture and the character of the God revealed therein.

The Change in Man

Once man had sinned, his nature somehow changed, for Adam and Eve suddenly saw shame in their nakedness (Genesis 3:7), and God saw the necessity of driving them from the Garden, "lest he put forth his hand, and take also of the Tree of Life, and eat, and live for ever" in his reprobate condition (Genesis 3:22ff.).

So what is it in man that changed? Edwards would succinctly state that nothing had changed; man's Fall was a matter of course, predetermined, and a product of man's nature as created.[11] But Calvin recognized that man, having sinned, was cursed with spiritual death. He was cut off from God's presence; which before had engendered, by its overwhelming qualities of goodness, holiness, and purity, corresponding qualities in the human nature.[12]

But it is Melanchthon who cuts to the heart of the matter:

> In the creation God placed a light in man, through which we might and should acknowledge him. With it we may still clearly know that he particularly loves us, and that we should

be his eternal Church, that he desires particularly to be active
in us in a way in which he is not active in irrational animals.
. . .

In the Fall man's powers were all impaired. The understanding was greatly weakened, and became full of doubt
about God and unable to know things as Adam knew them
before the Fall.

And just as the Holy Spirit before the Fall activated a burning love and joy toward God in the will and heart . . . when
the Holy Spirit was removed, false flames and pernicious
sores grew in the will and heart."[13]

It was the Holy Spirit, Melanchthon maintained, that made the difference. It
was the indwelling Spirit that kept him in touch with his God and enabled
him to attain to holiness. When he rebelled, the Spirit was withdrawn, and
mankind was laid bare before the basest part of his human nature and made
helpless to the wiles of Satan.

But with Christ has come "the acceptable year of the Lord" (Luke 4:19).
Those who have received the gift of the Spirit have been restored to fellowship with God. Their spirits have been *quickened*, made alive again, by
God's Spirit (Ephesians 2:1, Colossians 2:13, 1 Peter 3:18). The Holy Spirit
bears them witness that they are sons of God (Romans 8:16; Galatians 4:6).
He helps their infirmities, expressing their prayers "with groanings which
cannot be uttered" (Romans 8:26)—and so much more.

We no longer enjoy the comforts and carelessness of Edenic existence. In
many ways we remain "fallen man." But through the Holy Spirit we gain
back some of what we have lost; and best of all, we are restored to loving
fellowship with God, the Father of all.

Notes

1. See Dr. John Taylor, quoted in Jonathan Edwards, *Original Sin*, ed. Clyde
    A. Holbrook (New Haven: Yale University Press, 1970), p. 189.

2. See Henry C. Thiessen, *Lectures in Systematic Theology*, rev. by Vernon D.
    Doerksen (Grand Rapids: Wm. B. Eerdmans Publishing Co., 1979), p. 114.

3. See John Calvin, *Commentaries on the First Book of Moses Called Genesis*
    (Grand Rapids: Wm. B. Eerdmans Publishing Co., 1948), pp. 93-95; see
    also C. I. Scofield et al., *The New Scofield Reference Bible* (New York: Ox-
    ford University Press, 1969), Genesis 1:26, note; and Thiessen, p. 154; *cf.*

Clyde L. Manschreck, ed., *Melanchthon on Christian Doctrine: Loci Communes 1555* (Grand Rapids: Baker Book House, 1982), pp. 71,72.

4. See Calvin, *Genesis*, p. 127; see also James Nichols, ed., *The Writings of James Arminius*, vol. 1 (Grand Rapids: Baker Book House, 1956), p. 525.

5. Edwards, *Original Sin*, p. 192.

6. *Ibid.*, p. viii.

7. Manschreck, *Melanchthon*, p. 45.

8. Calvin, *Genesis*, p. 127.

9. See Jonathan Edwards, *Freedom of the Will*, ed. Paul Ramsey (New Haven: Yale University Press, 1970), pp. 239, 257.

10. Nichols, *Arminius*, p. 524.

11. See Edwards, *Freedom*, pp. 239, 257.

12. See Calvin, *Genesis*, p. 127; and Calvin, *Commentaries on the Epistle of Paul the Apostle to the Romans* (Grand Rapids: Wm. B. Eerdmans Publishing Co., 1948), pp. 67-83.

13. Manschreck, pp. 73,74.

Chapter 5.   Meet the Holy Spirit[*]

On the Day of Pentecost, God inaugurated the Church Age by the outpouring of the Holy Spirit "upon all flesh." This "Baptism in the Holy Spirit" was not an end in itself, it was only the beginning—the beginning of the Church, in which "this Gospel shall be preached" (Matthew 24:14, 26:13; Mark 14:9) and against which the gates of hell shall not stand (Matthew 16:18).

But Pentecost was also the beginning of the believer's spirit life in Christ, a life that is to be lived "in the Spirit." God never meant for believers to live without the power of the Holy Spirit working in them and outworking through them in gifts and fruit from the Spirit. Yet the majority of those who name the name of Christ today either (1) are ignorant about the working of the Holy Spirit, (2) do not care, or (3) neglect this vital resource provided by Jesus Christ for his Church. Even among Pentecostals, who ascribe to belief in the Spirit's power, there is a great gulf of ignorance, apathy, and neglect.

In an extensive survey of Assemblies of God believers, it was reported that only 67 percent claimed to have spoken in tongues at any time, while just 40 percent claimed to speak in tongues regularly.[1] Further, an official report reveals that, in the period 1982-92, almost 4 out of 5 new converts have not reported receiving the Baptism in the Holy Spirit.[2]

Of course, surveys cannot account for the genuineness of individual claims to being filled with the Spirit. Then there is the question whether all those who have once experienced the power and person of God's Holy Spirit have gone on to cultivate or maintain the closeness of that relationship. As John A. Wilson remarks, "In response to, `Are you filled with the Spirit?' some people will answer yes because they spoke in tongues at church camp or during a close encounter with the Lord. But does that mean they are filled with the Spirit today? Not necessarily."[3]

Bill Perkins, writer for *Today in the Word* (Moody Bible Institute) used the Texas Oil Rush that began at Spindletop in 1901 as a good illustration of those people who neglect to make use of God's provision:

---

[*] Chapter 1 of *Christ Within You! The Indwelling of the Holy Spirit*, published by the author, 1993.

Given this incredible resource, how silly it would have been for the oil field workers simply to cap off Spindletop and then move on, looking for another and better source of oil to meet their expectations! But that's what many people do in the spiritual realm. They look at Christ, the ever-flowing supply for their spiritual needs, but turn away and seek fulfillment elsewhere.[4]

This book is not meant to *teach* people the Baptism in the Holy Spirit, since the Baptism cannot be taught, only *received*. It is also not intended to teach *speaking in tongues*, since true tongues come from God, not the human mind, and thus cannot be taught. But it is definitely intended to teach *about* the Baptism, and to emphasize the importance, the benefits, and the absolute necessity of receiving the Holy Spirit in his power and making him the driving force in one's life.

I think of this book as a "workbook." I encourage the reader not just to become aware of its contents by a superficial reading, but to *work with it*. Write notes in it. Mark it up. Place question marks beside things you do not understand. Work out your beliefs as informed by the Bible, God's revealed Word, and let the Holy Spirit work by his "still small voice" upon you. And hopefully, after this open-hearted reading, the Spirit-filled believer will know "the way of God more perfectly" (Acts 18:26), and anyone who is not Spirit filled will be encouraged to both seek and to receive God's precious gift, the Comforter.

Notes

1. Margaret M. Poloma, *The Assemblies of God at the Crossroads: Charisma and Institutional Dilemmas* (Knoxville, TN: University of Tennessee Press, 1989), pp. 7, 12.

2. *Report of the Spiritual Life Committee to the 45th General Council of the Assemblies of God*, published as "Are We On Course?" *Pentecostal Evangel* (October 17, 1993):4.

3. John A. Wilson, "Are You Filled with the Holy Spirit?" *Pentecostal Evangel* (November 5, 1989):4.

4. Bill Perkins, devotion for August 16 (Colossians 2:6-10), *Today in the Word* (August 1993): 21.

Chapter 6.   Who Is the Holy Spirit?*

When the Apostle Paul first arrived at Ephesus, he found a group of believers already there; but they only knew about John the Baptist's message, the "Baptism of Repentance." When Paul asked, "Have you received the Holy Spirit since you believed?" they replied, "We have not so much as heard whether there is any Holy Spirit" (Acts 19:2).

Likewise, many believers today have never been introduced to the Holy Spirit, and know little or nothing about him.

There are many opinions regarding the nature of the Holy Spirit. Some think the term is just another name for God the Father, others that the Spirit is just an impersonal force that comes from God. Some groups have revived the ancient heresy of *modalism*, which holds that God himself came to earth in the person of Jesus, then changed himself into the Spirit (thus progressing through three "modes"). None of the above positions is scripturally accurate.

A Person of the Trinity

No one fully understands the Godhead or Trinity, the "Three in One," because God did not choose to fully disclose his nature in his Word. However, Scripture clearly reveals a Godhead of three persons: Father, Son, and Holy Spirit:

> *"I have not spoken in secret from the beginning; from the beginning of time, there I was; and now the Lord God, and his Spirit have sent me"* (prophetic of the Son, Isaiah 48:16).

> *"And I will pray to the Father, and He shall give you another Comforter* [like myself], *that He might remain with you forever: the Spirit of Truth . . . "* (John 14:16-17).

> *"Therefore, go and teach all nations, baptizing them in the name of the Father, and of the Son, and of the Holy Spirit"* (Matthew 28:19).

---

* Chapter 2 of *Christ Within You! The Indwelling of the Holy Spirit*, published by the author, 1993.

"Chosen according to the plan of God, the Father, through sanctification of the Spirit, for the purpose of obedience and the sprinkling of the blood of Jesus Christ . . . ." (1 Peter 1:2).

"May the grace of the Lord Jesus Christ, and the love of God, and the communion of the Holy Spirit be with you all. Amen" (2 Corinthians 13:14).

"How much more shall the blood of Christ, who through the eternal Spirit offered himself without spot to God, purge your conscience from dead works to serve the living God?" (Hebrews 9:14, KJV).

These and many other passages of Scripture clearly demonstrate that there is not only a Trinity or triune Godhead, but that the Holy Spirit is indeed a *person* and not, as some believe, just an impersonal force. How else can the Spirit be "another Comforter like myself," as Jesus literally said (John 14:16); how else can the Spirit "commune" with us? (2 Corinthians 13:14); how else can the Spirit be eternal? (Hebrews 9:14); and why does the Spirit so readily find a place alongside the Father and the Son?

Subject to the Father and the Son

While all three members of the Godhead are ascribed the divine nature, Scripture reveals a very definite hierarchy (order of authority) within the Trinity. God the Father is the ultimate Creator and authority of the universe. It is the Father from whom the mandates of his commandments come, and whose presence is guarded and worshiped by his angels.

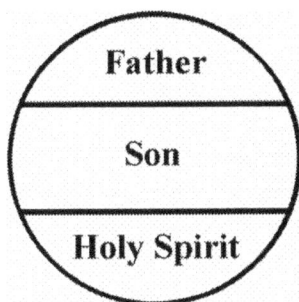

Figure 1. The Trinity. Though three in one, a definite hierarchy of authority is evident.

It is the author's opinion that Christ the Son and the Holy Spirit are voluntarily in subjection to the Father. It is their joy to submit and to serve, as it is the joy of the angels to do the will of the Father—and should be our joy, as well.

The Son serves in the role of God's *special* (*i.e.*, "unbegotten") Son, by whom God has chosen to show his love to mankind. What greater sacrifice could God make in order to show his love, an offering of himself or an offering of his beloved Son? Christ the Son, dwelling with God in an exalted state, through whom God created the world, voluntarily laid aside his divinity, and eventually his very life, in subjection to God and to God's Creation. There was no greater sacrifice that God or the Son could make. I imagine a scene much like that in Isaiah, chapter 6: God presents the great need for the salvation of the world. He asks, "Whom shall I send, and who will go for us?" (Isaiah 6:8). But this time it is Jesus, rather than Isaiah, who stands and cries, "Here I am; send me!"

Crucified but rising in victory over sin, the Son is exalted by his Father to the right hand of God's throne. God has "put all things under his feet," meaning that God the Father has granted his own power and authority over the world and the Church to Christ. Thus He is mighty to save and to provide supernatural gifts for his Bride, that they might walk in the power of the Spirit.

The Spirit, one concludes, makes himself subject not only to the Father but to the Son. The world *was created by* the will and word of the Father, *through the authority and power* bestowed on the Son (in the promise of his victory), *by the instrument of* his Holy Spirit. The order of the Godhead in terms of authority is thus Father, Son, Holy Spirit.

The "Hands" of God

The Holy Spirit is the workman of God, the instrument by which God (and Christ the Son) work. This is made quite clear from the first, as it was the Spirit that hovered over the waters of Creation (Genesis 1:2). An unnamed psalmist writes, "Thou sendest forth thy Spirit, they are created . . ." (Psalm 104:30), and Elihu declares, "The Spirit of God hath made me, and the breath of the Almighty hath given me life" (Job 33:4).

The Holy Spirit is the prophetic voice that speaks through men (and even a donkey in the case of Balaam, Numbers 22:28-30). The Spirit empowers men to do mighty deeds, as with Samson. It is the Spirit that stirs up men's hearts, gives them special endowments of wisdom and knowledge, teaches them the deep things of God, reveals secrets, warns of danger, heals, and performs miracles. The Spirit convicts men's hearts of sin, yet is also able to purge them of that sin and turn them into worthy vessels, trees that bear good fruit.

The Sanctifier (Who Makes Us Holy)

Jesus Christ has sanctified Christians, in an instantaneous sense, by his atoning self-sacrifice. When one places his faith in that sacrifice, he is saved. God counts us as holy because Christ has covered our guilt with his holiness;

but in a progressive sense, the Holy Spirit continues to sanctify believers by working in their hearts, changing them little by little as they walk in the Spirit. As Paul declared, "Walk in the Spirit, and you shall not fulfill the lust of the flesh" (Galatians 5:16). Then we can be "changed into the same image [as Jesus] from glory to glory, even as by the Spirit of the Lord" (2 Corinthians 3:18).

Greater Than the Angels

Many Christians have a great fascination for the work of angelic beings. But Scripture suggests that angels are created to work largely in the spiritual, not the natural realm. Angels worship in God's presence, guard his holiness, and oppose the evil spirits of Satan. When angels appear in the natural, earthly realm, they seem generally to appear to persons who do not have the Spirit of God, or to believers whom God wants to reach but are simply not listening. By way of examples: the angel of the Lord appeared to Moses in the burning bush when Moses was yet to know God in a personal way. Only later was Moses filled with God's Spirit, and was at times privileged to stand in God's presence (though cloaked by a spiritual cloud) and to speak to him "face to face." Balaam was at one time a true prophet of God. But he was corrupted by greed for what King Balak could pay him. When God could not get through to him by his Spirit, He spoke to him through Balaam's donkey. Only then was Balaam able to perceive the angel standing in the pathway, his sword drawn, ready to "part his hair." It was an angel that appeared to Gideon as he threshed wheat in secret for fear of the Midianites. Gideon thought nothing of his ability to be the deliverer of his people. But the Spirit of God made him the "mighty man of valor" that the angel predicted (Judges 6-8).

Christians today should stop looking for angels and following after other vain imaginations. Paul told the Galatians that even if he or an angel appeared to them and preached any Gospel other than that of Christ, they should not believe it (Galatians 1:8-9). God did not intend for Christians to look to angels as mediators, but to come before him directly by the Spirit that Jesus Christ has provided for us (Colossians 2:18).

Chapter 7.   Who Gives the Holy Spirit?[*]

The night before He was betrayed, Jesus comforted his disciples, tried to prepare them for the coming ordeal, and gave them important teachings for the Church Age. Foremost among these teachings was his promise to send "another Paraclete (Comforter)" who would "abide with you forever" (John 14:16).

Jesus mentions a number of things that this Comforter, the Holy Spirit, will do. These things define the Spirit's role and character. He will:

- Enable you to do "greater works than these" (John 14:12)
- "Abide with you forever" (14:16)
- Dwell "with you, and shall be in you" (14:17)
- "Teach you all things" (14:26)
- "Bring all things to your remembrance" (14:26)
- "Testify of me [Jesus]" (15:26)
- "Convict the world of sin, righteousness, and judgment" (16:8)
- "Guide you into all truth" (16:13)
- "Not speak of himself, but whatever He shall hear, He shall speak" (16:13)
- "Show you things to come" (16:13)
- "Glorify me" (16:14)
- "Receive from me, and show it unto you" (16:14, 15)

But Jesus said, "It is expedient for you that I go away; for if I do not go away, the Paraclete will not come unto you" (John 16:7). The Holy Spirit could not come until Jesus was gone. Why is that?

---

[*] Chapter 3 of *Christ Within You! The Indwelling of the Holy Spirit*, published by the author, 1993.

The answer is that Jesus was to be the *giver* of the Holy Spirit. That giving of the Spirit, in God's plan, was to be done not by Jesus in the flesh, who was yet to bear the sins of the world, but by the glorified Christ who had conquered hell and the grave.

How was Christ to be glorified? First of all, by his noble earthly ministry, proclaiming "the acceptable year of the Lord" (Isaiah 61:1-2, Luke 4:18) to the world. Second, by bearing the sins of the world to the cross. Third, by overcoming the bonds of hell in his resurrection. Fourth, by ascending to heaven. And finally, by being exalted to the right hand of the throne of God the Father, receiving from him all power and authority, and being given the ability to intercede and provide spiritual gifts for his Church.

Christ's Exaltation is often expressed by Paul by the term *fullness*. Christ has been made *full*, and is now able to *fill* his Church by *filling* it with the Holy Spirit (John 1:16; Ephesians 1:23, 3:19, 4:13; Colossians 1:19, 2:9).

This exaltation of Christ is clearly outlined in Ephesians (notice the key words "give," "gift," and "fill," together with an emphasis on ascending and descending):

> *Each of us has been* **given** *grace according to the measure of the* **gift** *of Christ. Therefore it says, "When He* **ascended** *on high, He led captivity captive, and* **gave gifts** *unto men"* [quoting Psalm 68:18]. *(Now He that* **ascended** *first* **descended** *to the depths of the earth. He that* **descended** *is the same One who then* **ascended** *far beyond the heavens, that He might* **fill** *all things.) And He* **gave** *first apostles, then prophets, then preachers of the gospel, then pastors and teachers . . .* (Ephesians 4:7-11, emphases mine).

These verses clearly connect the idea of *gifts* with the Exaltation ("ascending") of Christ. However, Paul here lists not the gifts themselves but gifted persons. Christ through his Holy Spirit provides the spiritual gifts of power that equip his workers to fulfill their offices. For instance, God provides prophetic gifts to the one who is called to be a prophet.

In the Church Age, *all* may prophesy since all have the Spirit available to them. Therefore, not all who prophesy can be considered to be called to the office of prophet. However, the one who prophesies frequently and whose prophecies are true can become recognized as a prophet by his works.

God also provides leadership abilities to apostles, teaching abilities to teachers, and so on. However, the gifts are not provided primarily for their own profit, but for the Church. In this way, those who receive gifts from the Holy Spirit can be considered to be gifts themselves.

This passage from Ephesians goes on to list the results that are to be expected from this giving of gifts to the Church. The gifts are for the purpose of "the equipping of the saints" (4:12) and so that "we might no long be children" (4:14). Results of the gifts include service, edification, unity, knowledge of Christ, increasing love, and ultimately spiritual maturity. The goal (though we can at best approach it) is to somehow achieve a level of completeness and perfection comparable to the "fullness of Christ" (4:12-16).

Christ, then, is the giver of the Paraclete, the Holy Spirit, in the form of comfort, gifts, and empowerment to the Church, so that it may be comforted and do its work of preaching the Gospel to all nations.

> *Go, therefore, and teach all nations, baptizing them in the name of the Father, and of the Son, and of the Holy Spirit; teaching them to observe whatever I have commanded you* (Matthew 28:19-20).

Chapter 8.   How Has the Spirit Come?*

The Spirit in Salvation

Jesus told his disciples that the Holy Spirit "dwells with you, and shall be in you" (John 14:17). This implies an external presence and keeping power of the Holy Spirit, but not yet an indwelling, internal filling. The full realization of the Comforter, Jesus said, would have to wait until He went up to the Father.

On the day of Christ's resurrection, He appeared to his disciples. After wishing them peace, He commissioned them to preach the Gospel: "As the Father has sent me, so send I you" (John 20:21). Then "He breathed upon them, and said unto them, `Receive the Holy Spirit'" (20:22).

This was not the full realization of the Holy Spirit. As Christ had taught, He could not send the Comforter until He had ascended to the Father in his exaltation to the right hand of God. Only after accomplishing that feat would Christ be fully empowered to intercede and provide gifts for his Church; but Christ had by this time accomplished the great work of bearing the sins of the world (at least those of all who would believe). He was now able to bring to them the Holy Spirit in saving power. The Holy Spirit had now come to be "in them," as Jesus had promised, *sanctifying* them (making them holy) in the instantaneous sense. The moment one believes in Jesus Christ, trusting in Christ's sacrifice for his sins and his soul's salvation, one is instantly sanctified in God's eyes. That makes one worthy to enter into God's presence. One is "saved." Christ has granted his holiness, which He earned, to sinners who do not deserve it. It is a free gift. It is "by grace."

> *You have been saved by [God's] grace, through [your] faith; but it is not for your own sakes—it is God's free gift. It is not because of [your good] works, or else some men might [be able to] boast [of their worthiness]* (Ephesians 2:8-9).

---

* Chapter 4 of *Christ Within You! The Indwelling of the Holy Spirit*, published by the author, 1993.

However, the Holy Spirit had not yet come in the progressive, maturing, and empowering sense as described in Ephesians 4 and elsewhere. He had not yet come providing gifts for the maturation of the Church. Jesus had not yet been seated at the right hand of God, where He has since been "given dominion, glory, and a kingdom, that all people, nations, and tongues might serve him" (Daniel 7:14). Thus the Comforter had not yet come in his fullness. The next step would have to wait for Pentecost.

The Spirit in Power

Jesus commanded his disciples to wait at Jerusalem after He had gone. Why, one might ask, must they tarry if the Holy Spirit had already come? Because the Spirit had not yet come in power ("fire," Matthew 3:11, Luke 3:16). The disciples had already been *baptized* (immersed, cleansed, initiated) with the water of repentance (John's Baptism). But in "not many days from now" they were to be "baptized with the Holy Spirit" (Acts 1:5). This would be their initiation into life in the Spirit, and the inauguration of the Church.

> *Behold, I am sending my Father's promise to you; but wait in the city of Jerusalem until you are endued [clothed] with power from on high* (Luke 24:49).

> *You shall receive power after the Holy Spirit has come upon you, and you shall be my witnesses both in Jerusalem, and throughout Judea, in Samaria, and to the ends of the earth* (Acts 1:8).

That endowment of power came on the Day of Pentecost, the Jewish celebration on the fiftieth day after Passover, after the disciples had watched and prayed for ten days. As 120 of Jesus' followers gathered together that day, a marvelous thing happened. The Spirit manifested himself in the sound of a mighty wind and the appearance of fire above their heads. The spiritual fire lit separately upon each of them, signifying that each of them had received his own endowment of the Spirit (Acts 2:1-3).

They were all thus "filled with the Holy Spirit" and began speaking in languages that they had never learned (hence "unknown tongues"). They were so exuberant in their praise that some scoffers accused them of being drunk, even though it was just nine o'clock in the morning (Acts 2:15). However, many foreign-born Jews who had gathered there for Pentecost declared that they heard these Galileans "speak in our languages the wonderful works of God" (2:11). The disciples had not suddenly learned the languages, but were receiving them directly from the Spirit (2:4). This "tongues-speaking" was the first spiritual gift bestowed on the Church.

"Baptism" and "Fillings"

This Baptism of the Spirit at Pentecost did not come once and for all. Pentecost was the inauguration of the Church, but there would be many more individual baptisms and fillings. The same group, and probably more besides, were all filled again (Acts 4:31). New converts at Samaria were filled with the Spirit with visible manifestations (8:14-18). Peter was amazed when "the Holy Spirit fell" upon Gentiles "as on us at the beginning" (11:15, see 10:44-46). The believers that Paul found at Ephesus received the same outpouring (19:6).

Old-time Pentecostals used to say that there was "one Baptism, but many fillings." Spirit Baptism is the initiation into life in the Spirit. It is the initial breakthrough of the Spirit's power into the individual Christian's life. The Christian must then choose day by day, moment by moment, whether to follow the will of the Spirit within him or "quench" the Spirit (1 Thessalonians 4:19). When one quenches the Spirit, the Spirit can then become grieved (Ephesians 4:30); but on each occasion that the Christian allows the Spirit to have free rein, he becomes motivated by the Spirit, permeated by the Spirit, and in that sense "filled with the Spirit." The Spirit fills him until he overflows onto other people.

Thus, the Christian receives the Baptism once, but can be filled many times. Peter, though first filled with the Holy Spirit at Pentecost like the rest, was again filled with the Spirit as he defended the Gospel before the Sanhedrin (Acts 4:8). Stephen, "a man full of faith and of the Holy Spirit" (6:5), was filled again just before he was stoned (7:55). Paul received the Spirit in Damascus (9:17), and was filled again in Cyprus (13:9). The disciples were all refilled in Pisidia (13:52). No doubt all these experienced many more fillings than were recorded by the author of Acts.

Christians should not seek to be filled once and for all. A single filling does not last because, put simply, "we leak." The most spiritual Christian, unless he keeps getting filled again and again, will cool off spiritually and sink back into the flesh. Paul admonished the Ephesians, "Do not be drunk with wine, which causes excess, but be filled with the Spirit . . ." (Ephesians 5:18). The sense of the Greek is to "keep being filled," a continuous or repeated action.

The manifestations and power of the Spirit were to be for the entire Church Age, in which we still live, to be a witness to the power of the Gospel and a resource for the Church. The Church needs this power. Without power, a church does not function as the Church. But God continues to fill receptive believers with his Spirit as at Pentecost to this day.

> *These signs shall accompany those who believe: in my name they shall cast out demons; they shall speak with new tongues; they shall pick up serpents with their hands; if they drink deadly poison, it shall not harm them; they shall lay their hands on the sick, and they shall recover* (Mark 16:16-18).

Chapter 9.   Who Can Receive the Holy Spirit?*

On the Day of Pentecost, Peter stood and preached his first sermon (Acts 2:14-40). He declared that this miracle of power and speaking in tongues was "that which was spoken through the prophet Joel."

> *In the last days shall happen, God says, that I will pour out my Spirit upon all mankind: your sons and daughters shall prophesy, your young men shall see visions, your old men shall dream dreams; and in those days I will pour out my Spirit on my servants and my handmaidens . . . . And it shall happen that whoever will call upon the name of the Lord shall be saved* (Acts 2:17-18, 21; see also Joel 2:28-29, 32).

Jesus once described the abundance of God's free gift of the Spirit to a woman in Samaria. Sitting beside Jacob's well, He compared the Spirit to "a well of water springing up" (John 4:14). This source of water was not a stagnant pool, but a spring of water gushing forth freely, welling up within the soul and satisfying man's thirst (see Isaiah 55:1; John 7:37; Revelation 21:6, 22:17). This provision, Jesus said, was for "whoever drinks of the water that I shall give him."

Jesus' cry is always, until the end, "whoever will." Today is still "the acceptable year of the Lord," the Age of Grace. Christ sends forth his message freely, and offers to all both salvation and power that is "mighty to the pulling down of strongholds" (2 Corinthians 10:4). He said, "Fear not, little flock; for it is your Father's good pleasure to give you the kingdom" (Luke 12:32, KJV). And with that kingdom comes the One who builds the kingdom of God in men's hearts, the Holy Spirit.

Peter's text from Joel makes it clear that God's provision of the Spirit is for young and old, male or female, mighty and lowly. Paul says further that it is for Jew and Gentile, male and female, and slaves as well as free (1 Corinthians 12:13, Galatians 3:28, Colossians 3:11). As for women, Scripture is replete with examples of women filled with the Spirit. These

---

* Chapter 5 of *Christ Within You! The Indwelling of the Holy Spirit*, published by the author, 1993.

include Miriam (Exodus 15:20), Deborah (Judges 4:4), Huldah (2 Kings 22:14), Isaiah's wife (Isaiah 8:3), Elizabeth (Luke 1:41), Anna (Luke 2:36), and Philip's daughters (Acts 21:8-9).

Between the Old and New Testaments, there does not appear to be much difference in the nature of the working of the Holy Spirit in the individual. What has changed is the breadth of the outpouring. In the Old Testament, the indwelling Spirit seems to have been reserved largely for a few prophets, priests, and kings. Certainly there were devout lovers of God, such as Samuel's parents Elkanah and Hannah (1 Samuel 1-2). At times, a measure of the Spirit was granted to lay people for special purposes, like the builders of the tabernacle (Exodus 31, 35-39) and the 70 elders under Moses (Numbers 11:16-17, 25-29). But the Spirit in power and revelation was not poured out to all.

Now with the coming of Pentecost, God announces his willingness to pour out his Spirit freely upon all. We would be sneering at God's gift if we did not only accept that which He has provided for our profit and the Kingdom's, but also seek earnestly to get all we can get.

Chapter 10. How Does the Spirit Indwell?*

The Nature of Man

The study of how the Spirit indwells the believer must begin with an examination of the fundamental nature of man: how man's mind works.

Man is a "tri-partite" being, meaning that he has three parts: *mind* (soul), *body*, and *spirit* (see Figure 2). Many experts think this tri-partite nature somehow echoes that of the Trinity, and corresponds to the image of God in man.

> *May the very God of peace sanctify you wholly, and may your whole* **spirit**, **soul**, *and* **body** *be preserved blameless until the coming of our Lord Jesus Christ* (1 Thessalonians 5:23).

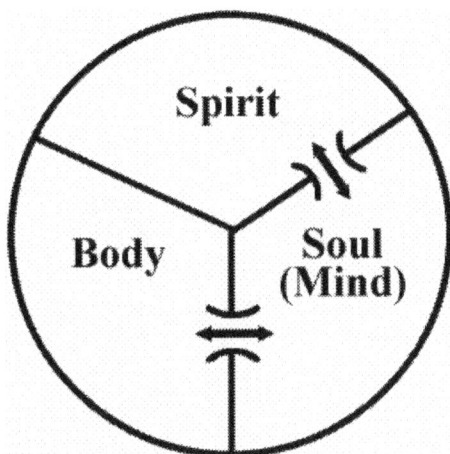

Figure 2. Man, a Tri-Partite Being. Man was created to have an active human spirit as well as mind and body. Information was meant to flow freely not only between mind and body through the senses, but also between the soul and spirit.

---

* Chapters 6-8 of *Christ Within You! The Indwelling of the Holy Spirit*, published by the author, 1993.

The Human Body

The body is, of course, the physical part of man. It is the containment vessel in which his mind and spirit reside. Without the mind and spirit, the body is a mere empty shell. Today, medical technology can keep the body's biological processes going almost indefinitely without the mind's presence or control. But without the mind, the body cannot truly said to be "alive."

It seems clear that the mind and spirit both reside in the brain, the control center of the body. Within the brain, electronic impulses jump from *neuron* (brain cell) to neuron, *synapse* (connection) to synapse. The brain's activity gives off energy in the form of brain waves, which can be sensed and measured by high-tech devices. When the mind and/or spirit is resident within the brain, this activity is also present.

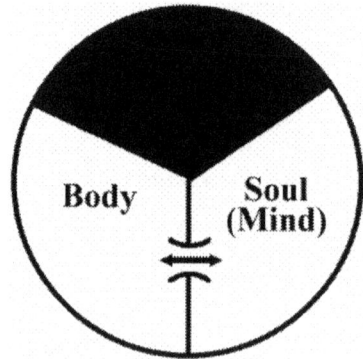

Figure 3. Carnal Man's spirit is dead or inactive. He is then motivated only his "soulish," natural mind. This is also true of the "carnal Christian," because he is not allowing the Holy Spirit to motivate his human spirit.

The Human Mind (Soul)

The mind is the soulish part of man. We often think of the soul and spirit as the same. But as the author of Hebrews asserted, the Word of God is such a penetrating "discerner of the thoughts and intents of the heart" that it is able to separate soul from spirit (4:12). The implication is that this would be a truly remarkable feat, but not impossible for God.

Technically and Biblically, the soul is the *mind*: the human, carnal, and natural resident of the brain. It governs all we think and all we are, apart from God. Because the soul so often allows itself to be dominated by the lusts of the flesh (the desire to please the body), Paul often refers to the soulish part of man as "carnal" man, who "walks in the flesh rather than in the Spirit" (see Figure 3).

The natural [carnal] man cannot receive the things of the Spirit of God, for they are foolishness to him; nor can he understand them, because they are spiritually discerned (1 Corinthians 2:14).

Even supposed Christians must continue to fight against the carnal part of their nature. Those who continue to sin are then "carnal Christians," being motivated by their own flesh rather than by the Spirit of God, and are considered mere "babes in Christ" (1 Corinthians 3:1-4, see Hebrews 5:11-14).

The Human Spirit

Man's spirit corresponds to God's Spirit. Adam and Eve were created tripartite beings, made up of mind, body, and spirit. But when Adam sinned, the spirit part of man died. This is, I think, the essence of Original Sin—not that we inherit the guilt for Adam's sin or of any other, but that we inherit the sin nature which is of the carnal mind, prompted by the lusts of the flesh, in the absence of Spirit-motivation. Or one might say that we inherit a "dysfunctional spirit."

Jesus spoke to Nicodemus of a spiritual rebirth:

Unless a man is born of both water and the Spirit, he cannot enter the kingdom of God. That which is born of the flesh is flesh, and that which is born of the Spirit is spirit . . . . The wind blows where it wills. You hear the sound of it, but cannot tell where it comes from or where it goes. Such is everyone who is born of the Spirit (John 3:5-6, 8).

When one is spiritually reborn through faith, his human spirit, which is dead, is "quickened" (made alive) by the Holy Spirit. That spiritual part of man is renewed, and the image of God that is imprinted within him is restored.

God has quickened all of you who were dead in trespasses and sins: in which in the past you walked in the ways of this world . . . . But God (who is rich in mercy, because of the great love He had for us), even though we were dead in sin, has quickened us together with Christ . . . and has raised us up together, and made us sit together, in the spiritual realm, with Christ Jesus (Ephesians 2:1-2, 4-6).

At salvation, God quickens one's dead human spirit. Then and only then is one's human spirit capable of receiving from the Spirit of God. The Holy Spirit then is available to quicken one's spirit continuously, if one does not quench the Spirit. It is incumbent upon every Christian to prepare his heart daily to receive God's instruction, guidance, and power from his Spirit, according to his will.

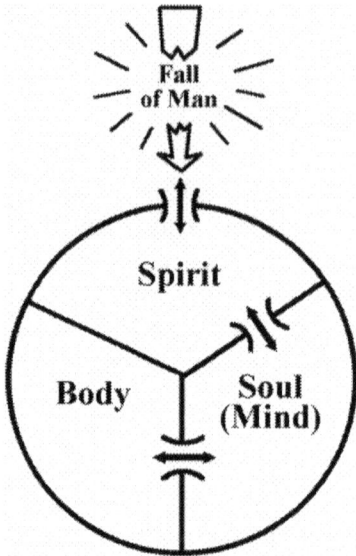

Figure 4. Spiritual Man is capable of receiving from God's Spirit through his human spirit. The Fall of Adam broke this relationship, and man's spirit died. But with salvation, man's spirit is resuscitated ("quickened"). Then Spirit Baptism enables man to once again receive revelation and gifts of power from the Holy Spirit.

The Seat of the Holy Spirit

There are many things about the human mind that the Bible does not go into, except by implication. But since, to use the well-known saying, "all truth is God's truth," it is not improper to appropriate truth from other sources, add it to the sum of one's knowledge, and use it to augment, supplement, and in some cases interpret Scripture. I refer specifically to the fields of medical science and psychology. One must of course be aware that in any discipline there are external influences, namely, biases.

Psychology, for instance, has to a considerable extent been corrupted by the humanistic and anti-supernatural attitudes of many of its practitioners. Nevertheless, psychology is, as I define it, "the study of human behavior," and as such can be very valuable in terms of determining how the human mind works and why people do the things they do. (This resource is not only helpful but essential for any pastor or Christian worker.) My aim is, at the same time, to recognize the biases and avoid them. The reader may be the judge of my success.

There is, for the most part, a scriptural void when it comes to the exact nature and operation of the indwelling of the Spirit. The reader is therefore fore-warned that much of the material in this section is theoretical. Nevertheless, I believe that the conclusions drawn are substantially true.

The Conscious Mind

When studying the indwelling of the Holy Spirit, it is still necessary to speak in terms of the human mind. That is because the human mind and spirit, while in one sense separate, remain inextricably wound up together. He-brews 4:12 has already implied to us the difficulty with which the two could be separated.

Man, as both psychology and experience show us, has both a conscious and a subconscious mind. The conscious mind is evident: it is the superficial part of ourselves that we present to others. It is like the surface and shallows of the sea. They are easily accessible. We readily observe the waves, the color, and objects near the surface. But the sea is very deep; the depths are hard to get to. Therefore, most of the depths remain unplumbed.

We all operate on the level of the conscious mind most of the time. The conscious part of ourselves is often the same as our image of ourselves. But the image is not always the reality. We all know people who think, on the surface, that they know everything and are always right. Yet in reality they are as fallible and limited as the rest of us, perhaps more so. Deep down, they might harbor an intense insecurity that prompts them to bluff themselves and others.

The conscious mind is pliable and sometimes unrealistic. It is subject to illusions, delusions, and outside influences such as peer pressure, desire, pride, intimidation, indoctrination, and propaganda.

The Subconscious Mind

Most of one's real self, however, exists in the subconscious realm. How can one prove the existence of a subconscious mind? First of all, when we sleep, we dream. Some people never remember their dreams, probably due to waking abruptly. Science, however, proves not only that the human mind continues to operate on a reduced level while asleep, but that its activity is necessary:

> Neurons die if they become inactive. The chaotic firing
> serves to keep the millions of nerve cells idling and alive so
> that they can be shifted instantaneously into gear in response
> to a stimulus.[1]

Dreams, then, might be the mind's way of maintaining itself while we sleep.

Second, many people report "sleeping on" a problem or decision and waking up, sometimes abruptly, with the answer, sorted out in their subconscious minds.

Third, most of us have had the experience of performing some activity, perhaps driving a car, and suddenly realizing we have driven an appreciable distance and made all the required turns, stops, and maneuvers, without thinking about it. We might not even remember the trip. We have performed the task in the realm of some kind of secondary consciousness.

Finally, hypnotism is the process of putting the conscious mind aside and delving into the subconscious mind. It is often used in law enforcement to help witnesses recall details that have been lost to their conscious minds. Unfortunately, it is also used for less legitimate purposes. Hypnotic methods have the potential to be used for putting things *into* someone's mind, not just taking things *out*.

> *Note: I discourage anyone, Christian or not, from submit-*
> *ting to hypnotism in any form. This includes such areas as*
> *psychoanalysis, transcendental meditation, creative visuali-*
> *zation, childhood or past life regression, and occult worship.*
> *It is highly dangerous to open up the subconscious to exter-*
> *nal influences that bypass conscious control. Failure to*
> *heed this warning might lead to external mind control and*
> *even demon possession. Never let anyone but yourself and*
> *the Holy Spirit mess around with your subconscious mind.*

The subconscious corresponds to the unplumbed depths of the sea. It constitutes what we really are, deep down. It represents one's true inner self. Like an iceberg, only a small portion of one's self appears above the surface, and only hints at what lies beneath (see Figure 5). Most of what we are lies deep within. Since the subconscious is where the real self, what we really are, resides, it only stands to reason that the subconscious is also the seat of the indwelling Holy Spirit.

Figure 5. "The Tip of an Iceberg." Like an iceberg, most of what we really are lies below the surface.

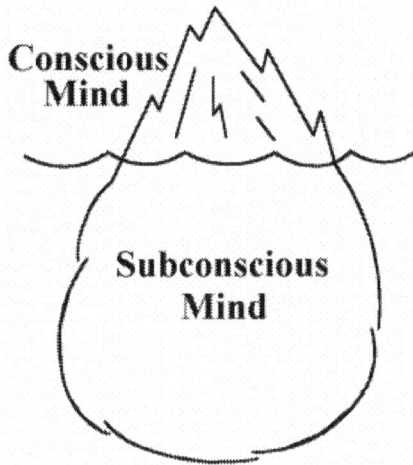

The Mind Gate

The mind has a natural protective device, which I will call the *mind gate* (see Figure 6). It protects the subconscious from intrusion. The mind gate is another term for the *will*: one can determine what is allowed to pass from the subconscious to the conscious, or to enter the subconscious from outside, as long as the fortress of the will is not broken down. I theorize that the mind gate protects even sinners, generally speaking, from demonic possession. A demon can enter the mind only if the control of the mind gate is given up or broken down. This can happen in cases of extreme degradation (*i.e.*, sin), insanity, drug or alcohol abuse, occult religion, hypnotism, obsession, brain-washing, and other effects that break down or bypass the human will. Sometimes people are led to voluntarily give up their will, as in the case of overtly satanic rock music.

The mind gate has its negative aspects, as well. Studies show that a person needs to have a free flow of information between his conscious and subconscious minds in order to be emotionally stable and well adjusted. Such a person, one could say, is "true to himself": he is the same on the surface as he is deep down.

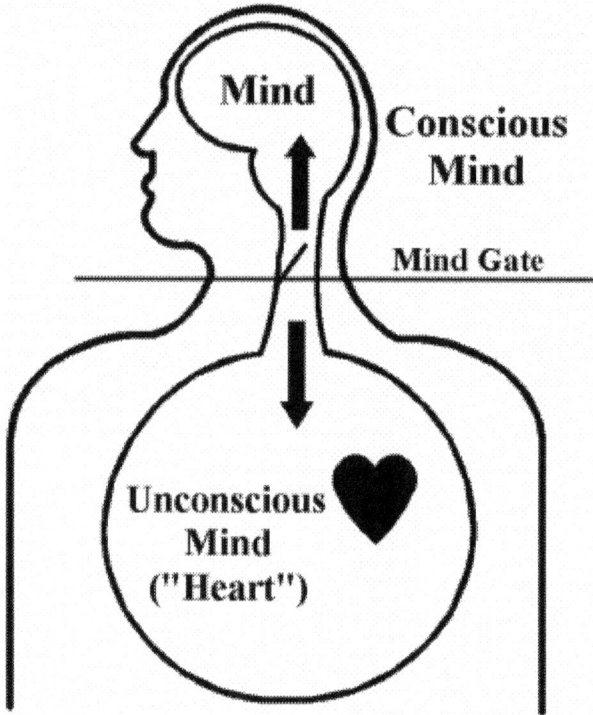

Figure 6. The Mind Gate, your will, controls the flow of information between your subconscious and conscious minds, and thus between your mind
and spirit.

When one is not true to himself, there is an uneasy tension within him. He
cannot be at peace with himself because he is at odds with himself. His mind
says one thing while his "heart" (which corresponds to the subconscious)
says another. By way of examples: one afflicted with *anorexia nervosa*
(typically female) might be malnourished but imagine herself fat. One who
ascribes intellectually to atheism claims there is no God, but on the inside has
a "God-shaped void," to use the common illustration. Conversely, a Christian might assent to salvation and forgiveness of sins on the outside but
harbor feelings of guilt and doubt that he can truly be saved.

These and many other psychological disturbances, caused by internal contra-
dictions, come under the sphere of *neurosis*. Other neuroses include or are
marked by depression, denial, anxiety, obsessive-compulsive disorders, and
phobias. A more serious state of denial or separation from reality may be
classed as *psychosis*. Some very severe separations from reality qualify as
schizophrenia (literally "split mind"); and a severe retreat from reality might
be the cause of many instances of multiple personality disorder (though the
possibility of demon possession should not be discounted).

Each of us holds the key to his or her mind gate. We must use the key wisely, but we should not be afraid to use it. One must swing open the gate often so that one's deep inner self, the subconscious, is exposed to the cold, clear light of reality. One must open the gate so that hidden fears, doubts, guilt, and grief in the inner man can be dealt with on the conscious level. One must have this free exchange of information within oneself in order to be at peace, and not "a house divided against itself."

The mind gate is our ultimate control over what we do, what we believe, and what we are. If the Holy Spirit indeed works in the deepest recesses of man's being, the subconscious, then you must first open your mind gate to let in the Spirit. As it is often said, "the Holy Spirit is a gentleman"; He will not force himself upon you. But once He indwells and becomes "Christ in you" (Colossians 1:27), you must then open the mind gate in order to let his gifts and fruit outwardly manifest themselves in your life.

Open Your Heart

The cry of the Lord Jesus Christ in this Age of Grace is always, "Open your heart." God will not violate your will until the Judgment. The Spirit does not at any time "take over" and make us do things we refuse to do.

Opening the Door

Salvation depends not only on Jesus' gift of Atonement but upon our choosing to accept it; we must also, as I have framed the scenario, open the mind gate to the Holy Spirit before He can use us to do his work on this earth:

> Behold, I stand at the door and knock. If anyone will heed my voice and open the door, I will come in to him, and will have fellowship with him, and he with me (Revelation 3:20).

> If you will truly obey my voice and keep my covenant, you shall be my special treasure above all nations; for all the earth is mine. And you shall be a kingdom of priests unto me and a holy nation (Exodus 19:5-6).

Unlocking the Gate

Once we have made the choice to let the Holy Spirit *in*, we must then choose to let him *out*. Scripture makes it clear that the Spirit within the believer makes himself subject to the believer's will (1 Corinthians 14:32). The believer is able to quench the Spirit (*i.e.,* "stifle" him, 1 Thessalonians 5:19), but is solemnly warned against doing so. When a Christian insists upon doing things contrary to the Spirit who dwells within him, he grieves the Spirit (Ephesians 4:30).

The indwelling of the Holy Spirit is a precious gift, and not to be taken lightly. The Christian receives a measure of the presence of God and thus becomes the temple of God. When the Christian sins, he profanes God's temple.

> *Do you not know that you are the temple of God, and that the Spirit of God dwells in you? If any man defiles God's temple, God shall destroy him. The temple of God, which you are, is holy* (1 Corinthians 3:16-17).

Cleaning House

God wants to work in our hearts to make us not only *be* holy but *act* holy. When the Holy Spirit comes to dwell in the believer at salvation, He wants to make himself at home. That means "cleaning house." He wants to begin by "cleans[ing] us from all unrighteousness" (1 John 1:9), purging us from not only active sin but the will to sin (replacing it with the will to do righteousness); relieving us of the burden of guilt for past sins; and healing the wounds and removing the scars caused by sin. This process, of course, is not altogether instantaneous; it is a continuing effort, and it requires our cooperation. It is all a part of our progressive sanctification.

Bearing Fruit

Then the Holy Spirit wants to break out into the conscious realm, to manifest his presence and nature in our actions. This is called "bearing fruit of the Spirit." Jesus said that if a tree does not bear good fruit, it is worthless. It will be cut down and thrown into the fire (John 15:6). We, like trees, are known by our fruit, and must bear good fruit or be judged worthless.

> *The fruit of the Spirit include love, joy, peace, patience, gentleness, kindness, faithfulness, humility, and self-control* (Galatians 5:22-23).

Breaking Through

The Spirit, one will note, does not violate one's mind gate to get in at salvation, and He does not pry open the mind gate to get out, either. One must throw open one's mind gate voluntarily in order for the Spirit to be manifest in one's life. Only with our cooperation is the Spirit able to bear fruit of the Spirit in our lives.

I contemplate that God wants us to notice this difference in the way his Spirit works in contrast to the devil's methods: Satan attempts to use pleasure, greed, intimidation, delusion, etc., to tempt or lure people, or when possible to force people to obey him through demon possession. The Spirit, in contrast, asks us to obey him with that "still, small voice" from within.

Unfortunately, throwing open the mind gate can be very hard and even traumatic for many Christians. I like to use the following illustration: imagine you and your life are a big house with many rooms (see Figure 7). Each room is a part of your life. Initially your house is all dark, its doors locked, its windows shuttered. At salvation, you threw open a door or opened a window, and let the light of Jesus Christ shine in. You felt, for a time, a cleansing and an infusion of joy.   Chances are, however, none of us throws open all the doors and windows of his life at that time.   The Lord knows the limits of our self-knowledge, self-honesty, and capacity for commitment. He knows that there are other areas He will have to address later, other doors He must knock on in time.

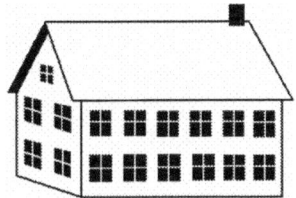

Figure 7. A Big House with Many Rooms

This might be the essence of the Baptism in the Holy Spirit. Salvation takes only a small measure of commitment, a tiny spark of faith in order to accept God's free gift. The Baptism takes a much greater commitment. One must open up many more doors, expose many more rooms of one's life to the light of Jesus Christ. Only then is his Spirit able to infuse those areas with light, cleanse them, and begin to work in and through them with power.

> *No man, after lighting a lamp, puts it in a hidden place or under a bowl, but on a lampstand. Then those who enter in can see the light. The eye is the light of the body; so when your eyes are good, your whole body is full of light. But when your eyes are diseased, your whole body is full of darkness. Therefore, be sure that your lamp does not leave*

you in darkness. If your whole body is full of light, with no part of it dark, everything will be full of light, like a shining lamp that gives you light (Luke 11:33-36).

The path of the just is like a shining light, which shines ever more as day fully dawns. But the path of the wicked is like the darkness: they do not even know what they are stumbling over (Proverbs 4:18).

The Lord shines his lamp into the spirit of man, revealing his most secret thoughts (Proverbs 20:27).

Those [seers, mediums] who do not speak according to [God's] word have no light in them (Isaiah 8:20).

God, who commanded the light to shine out of darkness, has shined forth in our hearts, [showing] the light of the knowledge of God's glory in the face of Jesus Christ (2 Corinthians 4:6).

Many Christians still have a lot of locked doors, areas of their lives that are still dark. They have withheld them from the Lord, refused to expose them to the light. He asks them again and again to turn over the keys, but they harden their hearts, refuse and reject him, until finally He quits asking, or his voice is lost in the din of self-interest.

In application, I see two contrasting scenarios: One Christian throws open many doors of his life all at once, and is immediately filled with joy and cleansing, speaking in tongues as the Spirit speaks through him, and beginning to manifest other gifts as well as fruit of the Spirit. This might happen at the very moment of salvation, as was so often the case in the Book of Acts, and still sometimes happens today.

A second Christian, however, must wrestle with himself and, like Jacob, with the Lord—"tarrying" at the altar for an extended period. He has a difficult time handing over the keys to his "house" so that the Lord's light can enlighten the dark areas. There are things he does not want to give up. There are dark recesses he does not want to deal with, relationships he does not want to mend. He might in fact keep "seeking" for days, months, or even years. Sadly, he might well give up before he receives the Baptism.

Note: Americans, on the whole, seem to have a much more difficult time receiving the Baptism than people in many other cultures. For one thing, we live in a nation that values image above reality. We also have too few avenues of self-expression and emotional release, usually limited to sports events, weddings, funerals, and other events in which emotional displays are acceptable. We are not "transparent," and have little tolerance for others who are. We are too concerned with what people will think about us if we "let go." We have too many "hang-ups." People in expressive cultures, such as those found in Africa and Latin America, seem to be much more likely to receive the Baptism immediately upon salvation.

This is not to say that the second Christian is not as serious as the first Christian in his commitment, but his desire for the Spirit has not outweighed the degree of his self-concern—his desire to maintain control of his heart and life for selfish reasons. While this desire is natural, it stands in the way of God's will. If and when that believer receives the Baptism, the infusion of joy and the feeling of cleansing might not be as great as the first's. He might be drained from the battle, or he might not have opened up as many rooms to the light, so that he is still "part dark."

The Baptism in the Holy Spirit, then, constitutes a breakthrough in the individual. It is a breakthrough of willingness and commitment, first of all, to let the Holy Spirit have control and flow forth in gifts and fruit; and second, it is a breakthrough of willingness and commitment to begin doing God's will rather than one's own, and to go and do whatever God might call one to do.

Until that breakthrough, the Christian might be "saved by grace," but he cannot truly be said to be "his workmanship, created in Christ Jesus for the purpose of good works, in which God has ordained for us to walk" (Ephesians 2:8, 10).

> *If any man builds on this foundation with gold, silver, precious stones, wood, hay, or straw, his work shall be seen by everyone, because it will be brought into the light of day. It will be tried by fire, and the fire will test the true nature [or value] of each man's work. If what he has built endures [the test], he will be rewarded. But if it is burned up, he will suffer loss [or be punished[2]]; he himself will be saved, but only like one who must pass through the fire* (1 Corinthians 3:12-15).

Notes

1. Gary Taubes, "The Body Chaotic," *Discover* (May 1989):66.

2. The translation of this word as "punishment" is very likely in the Greek, according to Bauer's Lexicon.

Chapter 11.   What is the Anointing?*

Before launching into a discussion of the gifts of the Spirit, it is necessary to discuss the concept behind the term "anointed."

God's Anointing

Literally, "anoint" refers to the practice of pouring oil ("ointment") over a person or thing in order to signify that he or it has been chosen or set aside by the Spirit for a special purpose. In the Old Testament, things could be anointed as well as people, such as the furnishings of the tabernacle. The thing or person that is anointed is then "holy," being set apart for God's use. When someone or something is called "anointed," in the spiritual sense, it means that God has set his mark upon that person or thing, accompanied by his power, with intent to accomplish his work thereby.

God's anointing is in some ways synonymous with God's blessing. God blesses an enterprise, first, by sanctioning or approving it; and second, by adding to it the power of his Spirit in order to bring it about and multiply its results.

God has always sought to use people in bringing about his will. He would like to bless his servants along the way, but if necessary He will use unlikely means, such as Balaam's donkey, to accomplish his Plan. In fact, God has on occasion anointed quite ungodly people to do his work. Samson's heart was far from God, and followed after his lusts. But God still placed the anointing of his Spirit upon him for the deliverance of his people from the Philistines (Judges 13-16).

When Israel insisted on having a king, God chose Saul and anointed him. He promised Saul, "The Spirit of the Lord will come upon you with power . . . and you will be changed into a different person" (1 Samuel 10:6). So, when Saul met a group of prophets who were prophesying, he prophesied with them (10:10). Saul went on to win many great battles against the enemies of Israel, in the power of the Spirit. Saul, however, took God's commandments lightly: God withdrew his anointing (16:14), giving it instead to David. Later, Saul sent men to capture David as he dwelt among the prophets at

---

* Chapter 9 of *Christ Within You! The Indwelling of the Holy Spirit*, published by the author, 1993.

Ramah. But when Saul's men approached the prophets as they prophesied, they were overcome by the power of the prophets' anointing and began to prophesy themselves. Saul came to see for himself, and fell down prophesying under the power of the Spirit (19:18-24).

God called the brutal Nebuchadnezzar his servant, using him to judge his people by taking them captive to Babylon (Jeremiah 25:9, 27:6, 43:10). Similarly, God called Cyrus, king of Persia, his anointed because He chose and empowered Cyrus to allow the Jews to return to their land (Isaiah 45:1); but it is nowhere stated that either ruler became a true worshipper of God.

External Anointing

Two types of anointing are evident in Scripture. The first is the type exampled above: an individual is chosen and empowered for a special purpose, regardless of his character, spiritual qualifications, or aspirations. Such individuals certainly have the opportunity to submit their hearts to God, but their personal salvation seems to remain separate from their assigned task. This type of anointing is often signified by some form of the phrase, "the Spirit came upon him" (though this distinction admittedly breaks down at some points), implying an *external* anointing that somehow "clothes" the anointed person. Such was the case especially with Saul and Samson. Many of the judges were described in this manner. The patriarch Jacob, one will note, was a chosen vessel not for his own sake but for the sake of God's promise to Abraham (Genesis 26:24, 28:13).

Internal Anointing

The second type of anointing is accompanied by a requisite devotion of heart. This type of anointed individual is more likely to be described as "full of" or "filled with" the Spirit of God; or, like Joseph, "a man in whom the Spirit of God is" (Genesis 41:38, KJV). When God sought a replacement for Saul as anointed king, He resolved this time to choose "a man after [God's] own heart" (1 Samuel 13:14). This is an *internal* anointing. Such individuals are "circumcised" (marked, committed, made clean) not only "of the flesh" but "of the heart."

The difference between internal and external anointing has crucial implications for Christians today. Jesus told his disciples,

> *Not everyone who cries, `Lord, Lord,' to me shall enter the*
> *kingdom of heaven, but he who does the will of my Father in*
> *heaven. On that day many will say to me, `Lord, Lord, did*

we not prophesy in your name, cast out demons in your name, and do many works of power in your name?' But I will declare to them, `I never knew you, evildoers. Depart from me! (Matthew 7:21-23).

Paul warned the early Church that some would come along who would preach the Gospel out of contention or for "filthy lucre's" sake (Titus 1:7-11, 1 Peter 5:2). There have been many successful preachers of the Gospel whose hearts were not right with God. Some are like the notorious Marjoe Gortner, who was raised from childhood to be an evangelist, but later denounced the Gospel and admitted that he had never believed. Such individuals have, at best, an external anointing on their ministry.

As Paul says, "We have this treasure in *earthen vessels* [containers]" (2 Corinthians 4:7, emphasis mine). Some vessels are not at all worthy, but God might use them, anyway. No doubt many thousands of Christians have been genuinely saved and blessed under the ministry of false teachers, because God's Spirit works in power in the Gospel, not necessarily the person.

Moreover, the devil is often able to produce false manifestations in an attempt to deceive unwary, unlearned, or unspiritual individuals. Christians need to realize these four spiritual realities: First, not everyone who is *used* of God is *approved* by God. Second, not all spiritual manifestations are of God. Third, being used in the gifts of the Spirit does not necessarily make one a better Christian. And finally, we have reason to hope in the realization that even though none of us is perfect, yet God is willing and eager to fill us with his Spirit and use all who have a willing heart.

Chapter 12.   When King Saul Prophesied

You learn more things by reading the Bible for yourself than you will ever hear preached. One thing I didn't realize till I read it myself was that King Saul prophesied. Yes, THAT King Saul. The one who threw the spear at David. The one who presumptuously performed a sacrifice because Samuel was late, and consulted the Witch of Endor. The one who sought David's life for years, and finally committed suicide.

Now I have long known that the Lord has used some pretty disreputable people. The brutal Nebuchadnezzar was called God's servant, and pagan Cyrus called his Anointed. It is often taught that Balaam was a false prophet, but a close reading shows that all of his prophecy was true. Only through bribery did he attempt to prophesy otherwise, but even then failed. Then there was that thing with the donkey.

Saul, too, was chosen by God for his purposes. Israel insisted on having a king like the other nations. God would comply by giving them a carnal leader who, like the kings of the heathen, would prove to be harsh and dictatorial. Rather than serving the people, he would make the people serve him. Yet God would provide for his people by placing his anointing on Saul as he did on the prophets.

Causing the family donkeys to wander off, God arranged for Saul to run into the prophet Samuel, who lived in Ramah. Samuel anointed Saul king and described several miraculous signs that he would experience on his way home. Among these was an encounter with a procession of prophets at his hometown, Gibeah, as they came down from worshipping at a high place. According to Samuel, "The Spirit of the LORD will come upon you in power, and you will prophesy with them; and you will be changed into a different person" (1 Samuel 10:6). Sure enough, Saul met the band of prophets and walked along prophesying as they did. Apparently, those who prophesied in this manner praised God and prayed as prompted by the Holy Spirit upon them. He passed people who recognized him, whence came the byword, "Is Saul also among the prophets?" The early years of Saul's reign proved to be a triumph over the Philistines, as God's hand was upon him.

Years later, however, Samuel had abandoned Saul because of his rebellion against God. A spirit would oppress Saul, upon which he would fly into a violent rage. Saul felt threatened by David and sought to kill him. When Saul heard David had fled to Samuel at Ramah, he sent troops to capture him three times. Each time, however, his men would begin to prophesy, apparently incapacitated by the Spirit of God. Finally he went himself.

Even before Saul reached Ramah, he began to prophesy. At Ramah he found Samuel and his band of prophets gathered together prophesying. Saul fell down prophesying before Samuel, stripped off his clothes, and groveled naked in the dirt all day and all night. Thus the proud king was humbled by the Spirit of God. Again, the people began to say, "Is Saul also among the prophets?"

You would think Saul would change his ways, but unfortunately his rebellious nature remained. Years later, he was defeated by the Philistines and met an ignominious end at Mount Gilboa.

Lessons

- When God speaks, everybody listens.

- Prophecy is more a work of the Spirit than of prophets.

- Those who would prophesy must humble themselves, or they will be humbled.

- Prophecy depends more on God's willingness to speak than our worthiness to receive it.

- God chooses imperfect, earthen vessels to contain, however fleeting, his glory.

Chapter 13.   What Are Spiritual Gifts?*

The phrase "spiritual gift" actually occurs only once in the Greek of the New Testament, in Romans 1:11. In all other instances, the gifts are referred to as "spiritual things" (*pneumatika*), "graces" (*charismata*), or a "manifestation (*phanerosis*) of the Spirit." My purpose here is not a detailed discussion of the gifts and their uses; other fine works on the subject are available. Instead, my purpose is to examine spiritual gifts in view of the question, "How do the gifts of the Spirit work in the believer?"

There are various lists of spiritual gifts in the New Testament, which look at the gifts from different perspectives. The list which I will use here is generally considered to be the most fundamental, 1 Corinthians 12:8-10.

Verbal Gifts

The verbal gifts involve receiving words or ideas from the Spirit and expressing them immediately and directly by one's vocal faculties: the mouth, tongue, vocal chords, etc. (though prophecies are occasionally written rather than spoken). These gifts include *unlearned* ("unknown") *tongues*, the *interpretation* ("meaning") *of tongues*, and *prophecy*.

The gift of tongues seems to work a bit differently from the other two gifts. In the case of interpretation and prophecy, the Holy Spirit places words, or more likely the ideas behind words, in the quickened human spirit. These ideas or words are made known to the mind, which dwells with the human spirit. Then the believer is free to express, voluntarily, those words or ideas in his own language, with his own natural voice.

One should note that the above gifts are expressed according to each believer's orientation. The speaker will not typically take on an accent if he does not ordinarily speak with an accent, or lose his accent if he has one. Regional colloquialisms (word usage and pronunciation) will likely be preserved. People who learned the Bible in the King James Version often speak forth in King James language, while readers of modern versions usually do not.

---

* Chapter 10 of *Christ Within You! The Indwelling of the Holy Spirit*, published by the author, 1993.

The gift of tongues seems to work more directly than prophecy or inter-pretation. The believer literally does not know the meaning of the words or sounds he produces. Christian psychiatrist George E. Parkhurst, M.D., surmises that tongues "is a gift of a language to a person's spirit bypassing the mind."[1]

To speak in tongues, the believer must yield conscious control of his vocal faculties to the Spirit. God's Spirit transmits God's message to the human spirit. To receive God's message, the believer must first open his mind gate to the Spirit, letting the Spirit into his innermost being. At the same time, he must open his mind gate in order to let the message out to the conscious mind, yielding mental control to the Spirit. The Spirit then actuates the parts of the yielded mind that control physical actions in order to produce speech. The sensation to the believer, according to reports and personal experience, is like water welling up on the inside until it comes bursting forth in a "gusher" of language.

> *Jesus stood up and cried, `If anyone is thirsty, let him come to me and drink. He who believes in me, as the Scripture says, "Springs of water shall flow from within him."' He said this about the Spirit . . .* (John 7:38, see also Isaiah 58:11).

I knew a young man who was marvelously used in the gift of the inter-pretation of tongues. But when the same young man "spoke in tongues," he became very agitated, and his "language" consisted only of rolling his tongue in an "rrrrrr" sound. I do not think that these were true tongues. First of all, tongues are language, not just sounds. Second, the Spirit is not lacking in vocabulary or variety of expression. Therefore, if the language is flowing directly from the Spirit, the language should change from time to time, and the tongues-speaker should be able to develop some fluency of speech. Fluency and variety are, I think, very strong indications that the tongues are genuine. The Spirit does not "give" anyone a "prayer language" in the sense that it is resident within him and available at will. True tongues must flow directly from the Holy Spirit and in a very real spiritual sense are delivered to the speaker straight from the throne of God at the moment they are spoken. If these observations are correct, then the young man, while (one might assume) being genuinely moved *by* the Spirit (with an emotional response), cannot necessarily be said to be speaking *in* the Spirit. His motives were good, but his transmission of the message was imperfect.

The above view is, of course, in direct opposition to some current schools of thought. There are those who teach that tongues become a resident faculty in the believer. The Christian decides what he wants from God and then visualizes it while praying in tongues. Such "creative visualization" is, however, a New Age (read "occult") practice. In many cases, adherents to this school of thought have also adopted the New Age view of themselves as "little gods" who, like God in Creation, can speak forth the creative "word" (whether *rhema* or *logos* is inconsequential, since the terms are essentially interchangeable). Bent on self-aggrandizement, these are often the same ones who try to apprehend the promised blessings of the future Kingdom Age in the present.

Self-deification, however, is unscriptural and incorrect. Christians are not made immortal in this life (1 Corinthians 15:53-54). Why else do we "groan" for our adoption? (Romans 8:23, 2 Corinthians 5:2-4). The Kingdom Age, in which Christians are to reign, does not come until Christ himself brings it, and takes his seat on his earthly throne (1 Corinthians 4:8, Revelation 20:4-6). If tongues are genuine, they come from God, not ourselves. The words are God's, not our own. Though the words might express our deepest feelings, it is the Spirit who frames the words, not us. Moreover, the Lord does not give us his Spirit to ratify our desires and plans, but to convey to us his own.

One cannot escape the conclusion that many "tongues" being spoken today are not genuine. While a believer might have once received the Baptism with speaking in tongues, he cannot rely on that one experience or the words spoken at the time. He cannot rely on repeating words he once said or once heard someone else say. The Spirit does not give us a few resident words that can be repeated like a *mantra* or "open sesame" at will. They must flow afresh from the Spirit or they are not *from* the Spirit, because the Spirit is "here and now," not "way back when." In the case of repeating words, the motivation of the speaker might be good, and the Spirit might be genuinely moving upon the speaker, but it cannot automatically be said that the Spirit is flowing through him.

One reason God gives prayer tongues (which Paul admits are self-edifying, not Church-edifying, 1 Corinthians 14:4) to all Spirit-filled believers is that they constitute the most basic gift: the flow of God's words through our spirits and out our mouths. This gift teaches us how to be used in the other gifts; for it clears a path for the free flow of the Spirit, and keeps the channel cleansed with regular use. We learn that when our language does not flow fluently, there must be a stoppage in the system. Then we can examine our hearts, our lives, and our motives, knowing that the stoppage lies within ourselves. In these ways and no doubt many more, tongues is rightfully the first and most fundamental gift.

Christians need to keep in mind two things about exercising spiritual gifts: first, the Spirit does not at any time take over control. He is a gentleman. The Christian must yield conscious control of his faculties in order to be used by the Spirit, to let the Spirit flow from within. Second, Christians must recognize that "the spirits of the prophets are subject to the prophets" (1 Corinthians 14:32). Not only can the Spirit be "quenched," but those who are being moved by the Spirit can make mistakes. One's own ideas can intrude themselves on the working of the Spirit. Heretical doctrines and practices can be the result. Sometimes emotions, which naturally accompany the moving of the Spirit, cause people to go to unnatural extremes of behavior. Some people might imagine that they have received special revelation or anointing from the Spirit, but are merely following their own ideas and emotions. We need to guard against extremes. As Paul admonished the Corinthians, "God is not the author of confusion, but of peace" (1 Corinthians 14:33, KJV).

At the same time, novices should be encouraged to step out in faith to exercise gifts without threat of embarrassment or censure. Christians can afford to make honest mistakes, and leaders can afford to make corrections gently and sensitively. It is the responsibility of more mature believers to teach immature ones, and the responsibility of immature ones to seek knowledge and experience in practicing spiritual gifts.

Gifts of Power

These include *gifts of healings*, *workings of miracles*, and *faith*. These are the gifts that produce the "signs and wonders" that Jesus said were to characterize and accompany the Gospel witness.

The gifts of power seem for the most part to bypass human agency and rely upon a sovereign act of God. By this, I mean that the gift does not flow through the human mind. Gifts of healings and miracles are not at any time resident in the believer: God does not give believers the power to heal or perform miracles at will. Instead, each healing and each miracle is a separate gift bestowed by God. God acts directly upon human diseases and circumstances in response to someone's faith.

All believers have a measure of faith. Even unbelievers have a kind of faith, and many of those healed in the New Testament had only natural, human faith. The gift of faith, however, is a God-given endowment of faith to believe God for the miraculous. The Holy Spirit speaks faith within the heart of a believer beyond his own human capacity to believe. Spirit-bred faith might be accompanied by gifts of revelation of God's purpose—to heal or act—that build his faith. The power of the gift of faith is that it empowers a mere human being to believe in a mighty way, beyond human reasoning, for miracles and healings.

Gifts of Revelation

Revelation is simply something that is revealed. A revelation of the Spirit is something that is revealed to a Spirit-filled believer by the Holy Spirit within him, absent of human agency. These gifts include the *word of wisdom*, the *word of knowledge*, and *discernings of spirits*.

The first gift is a "word" of wisdom, not wisdom itself. Wisdom is something that must be cultivated through knowledge and experience. "Godly wisdom" is, then, more properly called a fruit of the Spirit than a gift. "Word" here means much the same as when someone asks, "May I have a word with you?" It is a single message for a particular situation or instance.

Likewise, a "word" of knowledge is not knowledge itself but an item of information given by the Spirit for a given situation. An example will best explain not only how these two "words" work, but the difference between the two. As Paul was returning from his third missionary journey, he was visited by the prophet Agabus (Acts 21:8-14). Agabus tied his hands and feet with Paul's belt and said, "The Holy Spirit says that in this way the Jews in Jerusalem will bind this belt's owner . . ." (21:11). Paul's friends took this as a word of wisdom (what to do), warning Paul not to go to Jerusalem. Paul, however, more correctly took the message as a word of knowledge (fact), informing him of what would happen. Thus a word of wisdom tells one what to do in a given situation, while a word of knowledge reveals a helpful fact without necessarily suggesting an action.

The discerning of spirits has to do with identifying the nature or presence of spirits which might be at work in an individual or a situation: whether it is of God or not. Some traditions believe it is important to know the name of a demonic spirit while one opposes it, binds it, or casts it out. "Discerning" is plural, signifying that each instance of discernment is a separate endowment of discernment.

The gifts of revelation, like the verbal gifts, are revealed by the Holy Spirit to the human spirit and then the mind. They provide information directly from the Spirit, as needed, which is beyond the believer's ability to otherwise know. Like the gifts of prophecy and interpretation, the believer has conscious control over the delivery of the message. Moreover, he is made responsible for what he does with the information he receives.

The gifts of the Spirit are wonderful and vital tools that Christ has given us, by his Spirit, for the work of the Church. We should, like Timothy, "stir up" our gifts and seek not just to *use* but to *be used by* any and all gifts which the Spirit might wish to bestow at any given time. We should not, like an automobile's spare tire, keep them locked up just in case we need them in an emergency. But like a spare tire, if they are not maintained, at the very time we need them most we might find out that they have gone flat.

> *Do not neglect the gift which was granted you, accompanied by a prophecy* . . . (1 Timothy 4:14).

> *I remind you to stir up the gift of God which was granted you through the laying on of my hands* (2 Timothy 1:6).

Notes

1. Interview by Raymond T. Brock, "The Mystery of Glossolalia," *Paraclete* 23 (Fall 1989):25.

Chapter 14.   Speaking God's Message

The Holy Spirit and the Human Mind[*]

Truth is just truth; you can't have opinions about truth.

— Peter Schickele

Pentecostals have differing opinions on psychiatry and psychology. Many reject the disciplines altogether. Psychotherapy, an effort to relieve guilt and adjust other mental or emotional disturbances through applied methodology, is indeed suspect. Even among its practitioners, it often incurs criticism for its inability to provide real, permanent, complete cures.

However, well-taken criticism of psychiatry and psychology from Christians is due more to the assumptions that often underlie their practice than to the disciplines themselves. At the root of much psychiatry and psychology is the view of man as a mere animal with no real spiritual dimension, except that which can be taken as a psychological phenomenon. Added to this is the assumption that the mind is purely a mechanism which can be adjusted or manipulated. If there is guilt for past or present sins, *excise it.* If there are feelings of depression, loneliness, an inner longing for a deeper meaning to life, *adjust them.* If there is psychological disturbance, *fix it.*

But the essential practice of studying the human mind—of psychiatry, the medically-related study; of psychology, the study of human behavior—is perfectly valid. If "all truth is God's truth," then the truths made available through study of the mind can and should be appropriated and applied to the human condition and to Christian experience.

The Subconscious Mind, Seat of the Real Self

The purposes of a man's heart are deep waters, but a man of understanding draws them out.

— Proverbs 20.5, *NIV.*

---

[*] Originally published in *Paraclete* 26 (Spring 1992):17-22.

Though one might argue with details, Pentecostals must acknowledge the fact of the subconscious mind. When we are asleep we are unconscious, yet we dream.[1] This demonstrates some realm of consciousness, albeit the realm of fancy, which is active while the conscious mind rests. Psychiatrists have dubbed this realm of consciousness the *subconscious* (or *unconscious*). The subconscious appears to work with considerable independence from the conscious mind, or at least it seems largely beyond conscious control. It also seems to be most active when the conscious mind is inactive or deeply occupied.

Most of us are familiar with various manifestations of the subconscious mind, if only we recognize them. Many people have had the following experience: You are driving your car along a familiar route or a stretch of open road. You have something on your mind or allow your attention to wander freely. You are not thinking about your driving, yet you remain perfectly in control and arrive safely at your destination. Then you realize that you do not remember the trip. Your car was driven and your actions were guided by some sort of secondary consciousness.

Other examples are rife: You are occupied with some business, perhaps with your head down and your back to the door. Suddenly, out of your deep concentration you become aware that someone has entered the room. Though not consciously seen or heard, the intruder is nevertheless perceived. Or you suddenly tune into a conversation or a news report to which you had not been listening, when a key word or name grabs your attention.

A final example is more controversial. Many Christians are suspicious, perhaps justifiably, of hypnotism. They fear it to be a relinquishment of control, or even an occult practice. But hypnotism purports itself to be a way to reach the subconscious mind. The conscious mind is "put to sleep" in a trance so the subconscious can be contacted—not unlike conversing with someone who talks in his sleep. Hypnotism is regularly used by law enforcement agencies to help witnesses recall details. Reportedly, witnesses under hypnosis are able to recall minor details of clothing, appearance, the make and color of an automobile, etc., which escaped the attention of the conscious mind.

The human mind might be compared to a deep body of water. The surface and shallows are easily observable: the waves whipped by the wind, the well-lighted levels immediately below the surface, the rocks and other objects that protrude near the surface. This is the conscious mind. But the subconscious mind is deeper, darker, and relatively unexplored. Its contents are not immediately observable from the surface and are harder to get to.

Yet, the subconscious depths actually constitute the major portion of the mind and the reality within its makeup. The depths are what the body of water actually *is*. They are more representative of its true character. Surface features are just the portion apparent to the casual observer. The human mind is a vast sea that we have only begun to explore. Of all the complex structures and processes of the human body, the mind is the most complex and mysterious. Modern science can tell us some of the things the mind *does*, some of the ways the mind *works*—or at least make an educated guess. But it still cannot tell us *why*.

The brain consists of an intricate arrangement of cells called *neurons*. Electrical impulses fire from neuron to neuron across *synapses*, much as a spark leaps across the gap of a spark plug. When a person sleeps or his attention is unengaged, the intensity and frequency of firing decreases but never altogether ceases.

> Neurons die if they become inactive. The chaotic firing serves to keep the millions of nerve cells idling and alive so that they can be shifted instantaneously into gear in response to a stimulus.[2]

Even when we sleep, the brain's neurons must keep idling like an automobile engine, so they will not die. This might help explain why we dream. Freud and his followers have postulated that dreams represent the working out or the attempt to work out unresolved conflict in our lives. This might to an extent be true. Many instances have been recorded of scientists, mathematicians, and inventors resolving difficult problems in their sleep, awaking with the answer. Creative writers are often encouraged to keep a pad and pen at their bedsides, lest an idea that comes to them in the night slip away before morning.

But such examples only illustrate that the mind is never really asleep. It is always working in some realm, some dimension; and when the conscious mind is asleep (or otherwise fully engaged), that realm is the subconscious.

The Inner and Outer Self and Mental Wellness

To thine own self be true . . .
thou canst not then be false to any man.

— Shakespeare's *Hamlet*

Experts today believe the subconscious mind represents the true inner self. The outer self, the conscious mind, is subject to illusions and delusions, and to outside influences such as education, indoctrination, persuasion, intimidation, peer pressure, and propaganda. The outer man might accept intellectually the principles of human evolution or atheism. Most Christians, however, would agree that inside every person lies a deep longing for God. Conversely, one might outwardly give assent to salvation and forgiveness of sins through Jesus Christ, but inwardly harbor feelings of guilt, despair, and the belief that he or she cannot truly be saved.

Unless there is a mental/emotional consensus in which the internal, real self is externalized, or in which the outside influences (preferably good ones such as Biblical teaching) are absorbed and made a part of the real self, there remains an uneasy tension within the individual. That person is like "a house divided against itself." Sometimes the separation between the inner and outer self becomes severe and debilitating. A deep disappointment or trauma may represent a situation internally unacceptable to the individual, which might prompt him or her to withdraw the real self from reality, in full or in part.

A state of separation between the inner and outer self—between the conscious and subconscious—is often marked by *neurosis*. Neuroses are outward symptoms of psychological or emotional disturbance. They might include anxiety, compulsive or obsessive behavior, phobia, or depression. Other denials and separations from reality include schizophrenia, passive aggression, compartmentalization, and rationalization. Studies show that the more communication that exists between the inner and outer self, the more well adjusted the person is. In simple terms, the person is true to himself. He (or she) has nothing to hide from others, because he feels free to let his true self be known. (We call this *transparency*.) But most of all, he has nothing to hide from himself. He is at one with himself, with no illusions, no dissemblance, no dysfunction, no tension within his own personality.

Though psychological studies specifically of Spirit-filled Christians are too few to be conclusive, they suggest that those who function in the spiritual realm tend to be very well adjusted within themselves.

The Seat of the Holy Spirit

In response to, "Are you filled with the Spirit?" some people will answer yes because they spoke in tongues at church camp or during a close encounter with the Lord. But does

*that mean they are filled with the Spirit today?   Not neces-
sarily.*

— John A. Wilson[3]

Many of the ancients believed that the seat of human emotions was in the
bowels, which are noticeably affected by emotional extremes. Similarly, we
idiomatically place the emotions in the heart—it beats harder when we are
moved. But we know scientifically that the emotions, along with the intellect
and the memory, reside within the brain.

When the Holy Spirit enters into us at salvation, where does He reside?
Experts declare we human beings use less than 10 percent of our brain capacity. While the Holy Spirit needs no flesh in which to reside, He does desire
to indwell us and leave his imprint upon our very beings. Perhaps this extra
capacity is provided for the Spirit to imprint and actuate our minds, that we
might know the mind of the Spirit and be empowered to do God's will.
Having said that, it seems reasonable to surmise further that the Spirit resides
not in the conscious mind, which is subject to outside influences and false
realities, but in the subconscious mind, the seat of the real inner self.

Raymond T. Brock notes that the *corpus collosum* functions to provide
communication between the hemispheres of the brain; or it can rather inhibit
communication in order to make information more selective. He suggests
that in verbal manifestations of the Spirit, the information can be made to
bypass the cerebral cortex, which provides for direct control, and use only
selected portions of the brain to operate the speech organs.[4] This sounds
reasonable. The Holy Spirit does not at any time take control of a person.
Paul makes it clear that the prophetic spirit of a prophet remains under his
control (1 Corinthians 14:27-33) and that it is possible to "quench the Spirit"
(I Thessalonians 5:19). It is in fact necessary for the gifted person to lend
himself to the Spirit, yielding his control, his free will that the Spirit will not
violate, to the use of the Spirit.

In order that a person speak God's message and not his own, then, it is necessary for the message to flow from within his true inner self, the subconscious,
bypassing his direct control. The message must then emerge into the conscious realm, where it is pronounced by his organs of speech. The speaker
remains perfectly aware of his actions and hears the message. The message
is in the speaker's natural voice and is shaped by his speech patterns and
orientation.[5] It is, in fact, filtered through his conscious mind, though he has
for the time being voluntarily relinquished control.[6]

Both delving into one's innermost being and yielding control to the Spirit can be difficult to the inexperienced. Most people seem to have only a passing acquaintance with their own subconsciousness. We tend to lean too much on the conscious and concrete. The novice does not know what to expect. A believer might feel moved to speak during worship, to the point that speech seems apt to gush out in a flood, yet he might hold back out of fear—fear of the unknown, fear of embarrassment, fear of being "in the flesh." This is natural; it only illustrates the need for practice and experience. The most important practice, or at least that which is available to the Spirit-baptized believer, is speaking in tongues in private prayer. Without fear of embarrassment or being out of order, one can experience the flow of the Spirit's words from within. One can learn to discern the difference between the Spirit and self. Most importantly, one can learn to yield control readily to the Spirit, opening the channel to the innermost self, and thus to the indwelling Spirit.

> The Baptism is the submerging of the whole being, including the mind, and tongues proves the submerging of the mind. Speaking a language unknown to the mind shows that the mind and whole being are at that moment subjected to God. What physical phenomenon would better prove the submerging of the mind than tongues?[7]

If the words spoken are truly flowing directly from the indwelling Spirit, they should change. The speaker should not be simply repeating the same words over and over. As the Spirit-baptized believer learns to let tongues flow more freely from within, he or she should increase in vocabulary and fluency and find that the language itself changes over time. The Spirit has an infinite vocabulary and knows all languages in heaven and earth. Why should we limit the Spirit? The believer who speaks only the same few words, though genuinely moved *by* the Spirit, might be sadly limiting his flow *in* the Spirit. The Spirit, who speaks a here-and-now message, deserves a here-and-now messenger.

According to an intensive survey of Assemblies of God adherents by Margaret Poloma, only 67 percent reported having spoken in tongues at any time. Only 40 percent could claim they spoke in tongues regularly.[8] Clearly, there is a lack of sound teaching or a lack of emphasis on speaking in tongues in Pentecostal churches today. If the Holy Spirit does indeed reside in the subconscious, the true inner self, then the one who exercises the verbal gifts, and all other spiritual gifts for that matter, should also be in close contact with that inner self. He or she should become increasingly well-adjusted, psychologically speaking, in proportion to the free flow of the Spirit (one might say more *edified*). The more accustomed an individual is to the free flow of the Spirit, the more readily he can be used by the Spirit in whatever gifts are bestowed.

Knowing more about the Spirit can help the unbaptized or ungifted person know what to expect, what to look for, and how to seek for the baptism and gifts of the Holy Spirit. If people in our modern American culture have difficulty receiving Spirit baptism, which does not seem to be the case in many other cultures, perhaps it is because we tend to deny our true inner selves. Maybe the very act of receiving the Baptism in the Holy Spirit involves to a large extent the willingness of the individual to throw open all the doors of his or her heart, all the hidden closets, to the light of Jesus Christ; the willingness to face up to the ugliest gremlins of past and present and offer them up to Jesus to deal with as He will; as well as the resolve to thereafter submit to the will of the Spirit to do his will and not one's own: in short, to hold back nothing.

The idea that the Holy Spirit resides in the subconscious and the manifestation of the Spirit involves a free flow from the inner self bears further study from the various perspectives, including the historical, the psychological, and the theological. That the theory carries implications for the entire spectrum of spiritual manifestations is self-evident. Perhaps manifestations such as the phenomena of "being slain in the Spirit" and "dancing in the Spirit," when genuinely prompted by the Spirit, merely demonstrate the free release of conscious control to the Spirit: the one resulting in a trance to the point of falling down with abandon; the other in an equally abandoned expression of utter joy.

Notes

1. Some people claim that they seldom or never dream. However, it is probable that they wake up into the conscious realm abruptly or for some other reason simply fail to remember their dreams. If one wakes gradually into consciousness one is more likely to dwell upon his unconscious "meanderings" and retain them in immediate memory.

2. Gary Taubes, "The Body Chaotic," *Discover* (May 1989):66.

3. John A. Wilson, "Are You Filled with the Holy Spirit?" *Pentecostal Evangel* (November 5, 1989):4.

4. Raymond T. Brock, "The Mystery of Glossolalia," *Paraclete* 23 (Fall 1989):25.

5. Speakers of prophecy often deliver messages in characteristic ways. For instance, readers of the King James Version typically deliver messages in King James language, while readers of modern versions do not. One speaker might declare, "Thus saith the Lord" and deliver the message in first person; another might say, "This is what the Lord says," and use third person, all depending on the speaker's orientation. Such individualisms, however, have no real bearing upon the message, if it is genuine.

6. This voluntary relinquishment of control is to be contrasted with that of voluntary demon possession, as in spiritism. Spiritists often report having no control or recollection of their experiences while under possession and only regain control when released by the demon.

7. From a reprinted article by the late J. W. Welch, "What the Baptism Really Is," *Advance* (August 1989):5.

8. Margaret M. Poloma, *The Assemblies of God at the Crossroads: Charisma and Institutional Dilemmas* (Knoxville, TN: University of Tennessee Press, 1989), pp. 7, 12.

Chapter 15.   What is Fruit of the Spirit?[*]

"Bearing fruit" is a Biblical metaphor for producing results. Christians are saved by grace; but we are expected, once saved, to live by what we believe; to work hard at showing God's grace to the world; and to abstain from anything that dishonors God. This all comes under the heading of "good works" (see Ephesians 2:10, 1 Corinthians 3:9-15, James 2:14-26).

There are several concepts of fruit in the New Testament. John the Baptist spoke of "fruit worthy of repentance" (Luke 3:8). He felt that true repentance would be demonstrated by both one's actions and one's attitude. Paul, James, and the author of Hebrews spoke mainly of fruit in terms of righteous acts and personal holiness (Romans 6:22, 7:4; Colossians 1:6; Hebrews 12:11, James 3:18). Paul, however, goes on to list nine fruit in terms of God-begotten Christian character: love, joy, peace, patience, gentleness, kindness, faithfulness, humility, and self-control (Galatians 5:22-23).

Paul adds the further dimension of Christian maturity. This is all wrapped up in Paul's teaching that the new believer is like a small child that must mature through time, growth, exercise, hard work, learning, and experience (in spiritual matters), in order to become a strong Christian who is not easily discouraged or deceived. Paul begins one of his greatest passages on maturation, Ephesians 4:7-16 (discussed earlier), "Unto each of us is given *grace* (*charis*) according to the measure of the gift of Christ" (4:7). Paul's use of *charis* is often very close, if not identical, to his use of *charismata* ("graces"), a term he coined to describe spiritual gifts. When Paul speaks of God "giving grace" to himself or someone else, he often associates the idea with the giving of spiritual gifts, especially revelation. Significantly, he uses this word combination in introducing a momentous passage on good works, 1 Corinthians 3:9-15.

The first and greatest fruit of the Spirit is love. Love is, to Paul, "a better way" (1 Corinthians 12:31). He writes, "Now these three things remain: faith, hope, and love. But the greatest of these is love" (13:13). Does this mean, as some say, that all the spiritual gifts can be done away with, ignored,

---

[*] Chapter 11 of *Christ Within You! The Indwelling of the Holy Spirit*, published by the author, 1993.

or depreciated, as long as one loves? No, the gifts are to be the Church's tools for service throughout the Church Age. We need them desperately! The reason there is such a lack of holiness, edification (building up) of one another, spiritual and moral strength, etc., is that the Holy Spirit is not being given free reign to work in the lives of most Christians, maturing, empowering, and teaching them.

No, what Paul is saying is that the gifts *must be practiced* in love. If they are not practiced in love (for Christ and for others), then they are being done for purely selfish motivations.

> *What, then, brethren, is to be done? Whenever you are gathered together, each of you has a hymn, a teaching, a revelation, a message in tongues, or an interpretation of tongues. Let all these things be done for the building up [of the church]* (1 Corinthians 14:26).

Conclusion

Few Christians seem to realize that, while Jesus Christ walked this earth in the flesh, He depended on the Holy Spirit moment by moment. Christ laid down his divinity when He came to earth (Philippians 2:6-8, Hebrews 2:9). In his Incarnation, He was subject to weakness, to hunger, to pain. He was baptized in the Spirit immediately after his baptism in water. He prayed to the Father. He worshiped before him. He sought for the Holy Spirit to move in him and through him. He had no power resident in himself, but had to rely on the Spirit's power and revelation (see Mark 2:8).

We have this same power available to us today. But we need to make ourselves available to *Him*!

Chapter 16.   Spiritual Fruit Must Be Cultivated[*]

Once I had occasion to mow a pasture that had been neglected for some years. It had various kinds of tree saplings that had grown up in it: pine, oak, hickory, persimmon, and others. I was told to save some types of trees but to mow down the rest. As I mowed, I had to quickly identify each tree by its structure and leaves. For the most part, this was not difficult. A tree is known by its fruit.

Likewise, the Christian is identified by his or her fruit: by actions, speech, sometimes dress, and the activities in which he or she chooses to participate. Such are the attributes by which one is judged, not only by other people, but by God. While Christians are saved by grace, our actions are also important (see 1 Corinthians 3:9-17).

In Galatians 5:22-23, Paul the Apostle lists nine fruit that are born of the Spirit: love, joy, peace, patience, gentleness, goodness, faith, meekness, and temperance. These are to be the attributes of every Christian. But what do these attributes mean in the real world, in daily living, and how do you get them?

Love

The Christian is to be a creature of love, so filled with divine love that it flows outward to everyone and is manifest in everything he does. Consider the loving homemaker who throws herself whole-heartedly into all the drudgeries of everyday living: cooking, cleaning, laundry, etc. She could complain about all the impositions upon her, but chooses not to. Instead, anyone who visits her home can both see and feel the love that permeates it. Her loving care makes her love manifest.

So should be the daily life of every Christian: selfless, serving, caring for the needs of others. Paul tells us that even the greatest of spiritual gifts are worthless if not practiced in love (1 Corinthians 13). I think of the words of the old song, "Others":

---

[*] Originally published in the *Polk County Enterprise*, December 8 and 15, 1991.

Others, Lord; yes, others;
Let this my motto be;
Help me to live for others,
That I might live like Thee.*

Love as a fruit of the Spirit can only come from God above. Man has a measure of love, but it is finite; it has strings attached; it depends on his own desires and priorities. God's love is infinite—it has no bounds.

The fruit of love is necessary for man to truly love God (2 Thessalonians 3:5), to love his fellow man (1 Thessalonians 4:9-10), to obey God's will (Matthew 22:34-40), and to edify the church (Romans 15:1-3). God's love grows within us as we set aside personal desires and needs, and let the Holy Spirit work in our hearts.

Joy

Christian joy is a favorite theme of Paul's epistles. Such joy does not depend upon outward circumstances. It transcends all tribulation and hardship (1 Thessalonians 1:6).

Since the Christian's true fulfillment is in his relationship with God, he can find joy and reward even in persecution—not that he is masochistic, but his devotion to the person of Christ is such that he takes pleasure in selfless service, knowing that Jesus is pleased (Philippians 4:11-13).

Joy as a fruit is only found by entering continually into communion with God (*i.e.*, "walking in the Spirit," Romans 8). This is the believer's sustenance and strength. Cultivate and maintain your relationship with the Lord in order to have joy. Put his will above everything else.

Peace

We hear of many lofty hopes of peace in the world today, yet earthly peace eludes us. The peace God promises, however, does not mean the lack of war and strife. We can expect trial and struggle to accompany this life (John 16:33, Romans 5:1-5).

Paul's view of peace includes two ideas: First, *unity*. The Church, as the Body of Christ, should walk in agreement. It should have no petty strife within it (Romans 14:15-21). The Church should build up its members rather

---

* Charles D. Meigs (1907).

than tearing them down. A lone Christian is like a single fiber of rope. He needs to bind together with others in order to have strength.

Paul's second idea is that of *inner peace*, a restful security and utter trust in God. This peace is achieved by walking by faith, not by sight (2 Corinthians 5:7), and by walking in the Spirit, not in the flesh (Romans 5:16). As Paul writes, "Those things which you have seen in me, do; and the God of peace shall be with you"; and then "the peace of God, which passes all understanding, shall keep your hearts and minds through Christ Jesus" (Philippians 4:9, 7).

These two things, unity and inner peace, work hand in hand. Through the God-given peace in one's heart, one is enabled to comfort other believers (2 Corinthians 1:3-5).

Patience

Patience, or "long-suffering," is probably the most desired but least appreciated fruit of the Spirit. You see, patience is not usually bestowed miraculously—it is *developed*. Like muscles, it grows strong through its exercise. In order to develop long-suffering, one has to "suffer long."

Patience is more than the ability to bear petty annoyances and put up with bothersome people: it is also "grit," the inner strength to keep going in spite of adversity, to get a difficult job done, to see through a trying situation; or sometimes to be willing to sit and wait for God's intervention and provision when you have done all you can do. Nothing worthwhile ever comes about but through time, toil, and tears.

Through Christ's long-suffering, believers have escaped damnation and been granted a share of God's kingdom (Romans 9:22-24). Can we do less than bear the yoke for him?

Gentleness and Goodness

These two fruit can well be taken together, since their meanings overlap. "Gentleness" (in Greek) connotes kindness, generosity, and goodness, while "goodness" connotes generosity, virtue, and beneficence.

Goodness and gentleness are vital to Christian living. Those who are unregenerate, separated from God, or walking in rebellion, tend to do evil. Those who are true servants of Jesus Christ, living according to his commandments and empowered by his Spirit, strive to do only good. They not only abstain from sin in order to maintain personal holiness, but also give attention to charitable deeds.

Christians should give aid to the needy, encouragement to the discouraged, comfort to the broken-hearted, and even return kindness for mistreatment (Romans 12:9-21). God's glory is best shown to the world by the undeniable goodness He has wrought in his people.

Faith

To many people, faith is an ethereal power wielded by spiritual giants, unavailable to ordinary men. However, faith at its purest is simple trust in God. Ask yourself: do you trust God even though you cannot see his purposes in your trials? If you do, you have faith.

In the context of Galatians 5, however, "faith" would better be rendered "faithfulness" or "reliability." God wants believers to be recognized as worthy of belief, reliance, and trust. This is what Jesus means when He says, "Do not swear at all, neither by heaven . . . nor by the earth . . . but let your *yes* be *yes*, and your *no, no*" (Matthew 5:34-37). The Christian must be as good as his word, for the sake of his witness.

In order to cultivate the fruit of faithfulness, submit to man's laws as a dutiful citizen; submit to one another as humble servants; and submit to God as a willing vessel for his use.

Meekness

Jesus washed his disciples' feet and said, "You also ought to wash another's feet" (John 13:14). Likewise, Paul taught, "In lowliness of mind, let each esteem others better than themselves" (Philippians 2:3).

As someone said, "Meekness is not weakness." It is not shyness or timidity. Meekness is the willingness to set aside one's honor, position, and power in an attitude of humility, as Jesus set aside his heavenly glory in order to suffer and die for our sins.

However, as pride set Satan apart from God, pride continues to separate men from God and from each other. Christians are to subdue that pride and offer it up to God as an act of worship (Romans 12:1-3).

Cultivating meekness requires walking in the Spirit, not in the flesh. It requires a conscious decision not to respond to others in pride and selfishness, or "to think of oneself more highly than one ought to think" (Romans 12:3), but to think and act in a godly way, and Jesus would.

Self-Control (Temperance)

Paul uses this term in two ways: First, he applies it to those who are tempted by carnal desires, especially sexual promiscuity. These he instructs to "flee youthful lusts, but follow righteousness, faith, love, peace, with those who call on the Lord out of a pure heart" (2 Timothy 2:22). Christians can choose what to think about, and what activities to pursue. Instead of being subject to carnal desires, we can choose to walk in the Spirit.

Of course, some will remain weak and in danger of moral failure. Fewer Christians would fall into immorality if they had trustworthy Christian friends who were willing to counsel and strengthen them in prayer and companionship. But one who is tempted can take concrete steps to avoid temptation. In the case of extreme sexual temptation, Paul suggests they seek to marry (1 Corinthians 7:9).

Second, Paul relates self-control to athletes in training (1 Corinthians 9:24-27). The disciplined Christian can better resist the wiles of the devil (Ephesians 6:10-18). Do not be slack in your spiritual growth, but spend time praying, worshipping God, reading you Bible, and ministering to others. A disciplined Christian makes a good soldier for Christ.

Conclusion

God earnestly desires that all Christians possess and exercise all nine fruit of the Spirit. They are not an option! As Jesus said, every branch which does not bear fruit will be cut off and cast into the fire" (John 15:6).

Right now, let us renew our commitment, and pledge to redouble our efforts to bear spiritual fruit for God.

Chapter 17.   Make Way for the Spirit!

How to Have More Spiritual Church Worship

As described in 1 Corinthians 14, there are few worship activities that are as edifying and energizing as the verbal gifts of the Spirit. However, in circulating amongst various Full Gospel churches in recent years, I have noticed an absence of verbal manifestations (messages in tongues, interpretation, prophecy) in most services. Some churches apparently go for weeks or months without hearing a fresh "word" from the Lord.

While prophecy in particular might be abused or over-emphasized in some circles, a church is ill-advised to react by trying to limit or control manifestations.

Sometimes pastors ask me what they can do to make their services more spiritual. I offer the following suggestions:

1. Pray Up

In order to be sensitive to the moving of the Spirit, the pastor or worship leader must be spiritually sensitive. Moves of God do not always come through the leader -- make sure you are on the cutting edge, not the tail! Fast and pray before each service, and engage prayer warriors to bolster that intercession. Be sure you are cleaned up, prayed up, and "fessed up." Set aside all unnecessary activities and distractions, and go into the service with your mind centered on the Lord.

2. Let Go

No one can quench the Spirit like the "man in charge." Do not let yourself be preoccupied with the order of the service. Never change the order when the Spirit is trying to move. Wait! Be secure in your spiritual authority, unafraid that you might lose control of the service. (If you do not have spiritual authority, GET SOME!) Do not give in to the conceit that the move of the Spirit always comes through the leader. Avoid trying to manipulate the people, dictating their actions, or trying to stir up the Spirit by human means.

IMPORTANT: Do not limit the opportunity to speak to a few chosen leaders. The moving of the Spirit in Acts and Corinthians is corporate and "upon all flesh," not limited. (As Paul wrote, "you may all prophesy one by one," and "let one speak, and let the others judge.")

3. Pipe Down

The Spirit does not always move in an atmosphere of noise and frenetic activity (which is prevalent these days). Moves are more likely genuine when they are spontaneous. Often, the Spirit settles on the congregation with a warm, sweet heaviness. Do not be afraid of "quiet times" or "dead air" -- avoid the temptation to fill every moment with words or activity. Do not keep the music volume so loud that someone speaking in the Spirit in the congregation cannot be heard! (In a large church, place microphones in strategic areas, and instruct the congregation on their proper use.)

4. Slow Down

I have often felt moved by the Spirit to speak, but had no opportunity that would not interrupt the order of service. Since I do not seem to receive an entire message until I have begun to speak, the moment was quickly past. Again, do not let yourself be preoccupied with advancing the order of service. Do not hurry through the worship time -- if it or any other activity were a mere "preliminary," it could be eliminated! Do not treat the Spirit as such. A true word from the Lord is probably more important than your sermon!

5. Teach and Preach the Gifts

Give proper emphasis to the spiritual gifts in the church, teach their appropriate use, and encourage members to seek them. (Even the best teaching will be voided if you do not then give the people adequate opportunity to exercise the gifts.) Allow people to make honest mistakes. Correct mistakes gently and respectfully from the pulpit when necessary, in private when possible -- keeping in mind the potential for public embarrassment. Realize that the gifts are for lay people, too!

If the above suggestions are followed, I cannot guarantee that a move of the Spirit will take place, but hopefully a lot of human barriers will have been removed, in order to encourage and make room for the gifts in the service. Is that not what is truly important?

Chapter 18.   Christ, Our Easter Lamb*

Beginning as early as Genesis, God used the symbol of the innocent lamb as an example of the Christ who was to come.

Technically, this use of prophetic symbolism is known as "typology." The spotless lamb is a "type" of Christ.

As a shepherding people, the lamb was a symbol with which all Jews could identify. They viewed the lamb as the embodiment of sweet, beautiful innocence, much as we would view a puppy or a kitten.

The prophet Nathan once told King David a story about a poor man who had raised a lamb as his own child. Unfortunately, a greedy rich man stole the lamb and had it slaughtered to feed his guest. David, a former shepherd, was incensed. He declared that the man who had done such a deed was worthy of death (2 Samuel 12).

In his Word, God chose to give us numerous pictures of just such an innocent Lamb who would be slaughtered undeservedly, sacrificed for the sins of the guilty.

In Genesis 22, God told Abraham to take his beloved son Isaac to Mt. Moriah and sacrifice him. At the last moment, God substituted a ram in place of Isaac. As Abraham had told his son, "God will provide himself a lamb for a burnt offering."

When Israel was captive in Egypt, God sent ten plagues upon the Egyptians to force Pharoah to let them go. In the final plague, God sent the angel of death to kill all their first-born.

But God gave Israel a way of escape. They were each to take a spotless, first-born lamb and slaughter it. They were to smear its blood upon their door-posts, and eat its flesh in a memorial dinner. When the death angel saw the blood, it would pass them by. This was the first Passover (Exodus 11-12).

God instituted various animal sacrifices as an object lesson in sin and forgiveness. When Adam and Eve sinned, God declared that every man would

---

* Originally published in the Polk County Enterprise.

have to die for his own sins. "The soul that sins shall die," He said (Ezekiel 18:4).

But through sacrifice, God showed us that innocent blood could cover our sins. Of course, the blood of animals could never truly pay for human sin. But those paltry sacrifices pointed to the One who would be the ultimate sacrifice.

On the Day of Atonement (Yom Kippur) came a truly special sacrifice. At this annual event, the High Priest would make a sacrifice for the nation as a whole. He would take two goat kids, one of which would become a burnt offering.

The second kid was a sin offering, called the "scapegoat." The High Priest would place his hands on the goat's head and confess over it the sins of the nation. Thus Israel's sin was symbolically transferred to the goat. Then the goat was released in the wilderness, to die in the wild (Leviticus 16).

Both these goats were types of Christ. The first died for Israel's sins. The second, the scapegoat, symbolized the carrying away of their sin, where it would be lost and forgotten. Like the first, Christ died for our sins. Like the second, Christ carried away our sins "as far as the east is from the west" (Psalm 103:12).

Christ could have called legions of angels to save him from death on the cross. But He had the ultimate task to perform, to die as the spotless Lamb for sinners slain, "who takes away the sins of the world" (John 1:29).

Christ submitted to this ignominious death. "He was brought like a lamb to the slaughter; and like a sheep that is mute before its shearers, He did not open his mouth" (Isaiah 53:7).

In the end, the risen Christ is triumphant. He comes as both Lion and Lamb before the throne of God. He alone is worthy to open the seven seals of judgment (Revelation 5).

Jesus Christ is the spotless Lamb who was killed on that first Easter for my sins and yours. Because He has arisen from the dead, He has conquered death and the grave. His sacrifice long ago has become an eternal sacrifice for all who will believe and follow him, now and forevermore.

"God so loved the world that He gave his firstborn Son, so that whoever believes in him might not perish, but have eternal life. God did not send his

Son into the world to condemn the world, but so that the world might be saved through him" (John 3:16-17).

"This is love: not that we loved God, but that He loved us and sent his Son to be the atoning sacrifice for our sins" (1 John 4:10).

We ought to love and serve, with every fiber of our beings, the kind of God who loved us so much.

Chapter 19.   A Little Bit at a Time

Jesus loved the world so much,
He was willing to leave highest heaven;
To come to live in a physical body,
To know what it is to hurt, to hunger, to fear,
To sorrow, to suffer, and to bleed.

He loved the whole world so much,
He was willing to be staked to a post,
Tormented,
To suffer for sins that were not his—
To die slowly, shamefully, horribly.

Jesus took me as his servant,
And made me a little bit like him;
He gave me a mission,
A heavenly call,
And sent me out to love the world.

But I was too small
To love the world so much—
So He let me love it
A little bit at a time.

Chapter 20.   Life to Live

A Minimalist Testimony

I stood on the brink
Of life
And realized
'Twas death I'd lived
Apart from God
From birth till then.

I saw my dreams
As waste--
Of hours, years
Self-seeking,
Now wishing so
To live anew.

My life I give
Christ Jesus
Atoning Lamb
For sinners slain
Choosing daily now
Life to live
in Him.

Chapter 21.   The Fullness of Christ

And the Maturation of the Church in Ephesians 4:7-16*

Christ did not ascend into heaven without making provision for those He left behind.   Sending the Holy Spirit to act in his place as Comforter and Teacher, Christ took his rightful place in the seat of power and authority.

But the presence and indwelling of the Holy Spirit were not the end of his scheme.   The individual Christian was never meant to stand alone.   Christ's intention was to build a brotherhood of believers, a Church, which "the gates of Hades shall not prevail against" (Mt. 16:18).   For this purpose Christ, through the Holy Spirit, has arranged for this Church to be created, organized, and equipped to its task by his providing apostles, prophets, evangelists, pastors, and teachers.

Most of the study of Ephesians 4:7-16 seems to have been centered in three areas: the definition of the terms apostle, prophet, etc.; Paul's use of Psalm 68:18 (=Eph. 4:8); and the description of Christ as having "descended into the depths of the earth" (4:9).   Without discounting entirely these facets of the text, the intention here is rather to focus on the nature of the result: The Church, receiving from Christ the leaders and personnel it needs for equipping and edification, is to somehow attain "unto a complete man, unto the measure of stature of the fullness of Christ."

Herein lies the heart of the matter.   Knowing Christ's purposes in regard to his Church, how do these correspond to the *fullness* of Christ?   What, in fact, is the "fullness" of Christ—is He in any way empty or incomplete?   Is it the Church's responsibility to "fulfill" Christ?

Delineation of the Passage

While the Nestle-Aland critical text[1] does not include a paragraph break between verses 6 and 7, the UBS text[2] supports such a break.   Even were that not the case, it would appropriately serve our purposes: verse 7 marks the introduction of the "gift" theme, which carries on through verse 16; after which both texts paragraph, and the theme shifts.

---

* Originally an exegesis paper presented to Dr. Donald A. Johns, The Assemblies of God Theological Seminary, November 20, 1985.

Textual Variants

There are few textual variants in this passage that have any bearing upon the outcome of this study. Nevertheless, two variants must be considered: First, the end of verse 15 reads, *hos estin he kephale Christos*. The variant here reads instead *hos estin he kephale tou Christou*. The question is whether we are to grow up into Christ or into God himself, since it is God who is the head of Christ. The variant is testified to only by Papyrus 46; which, though considered a significant manuscript, does not by itself weigh heavily enough against the others. Furthermore, the text of Ephesians has already spoken of Christ as head of his Body, the Church (1:20-23), and named its goal as attaining the stature of Christ (4:13).

Second, the end of verse 16 reads *eis oikodomen heautou*, referring to the Body, while the variant reads *eis oikodomen autou*. The variant is testified to most importantly by Codex *Sinaiticus*, while Papyrus 46, *Alexandrinus*, *Vaticanus*, and others weigh against it. The variant's significance is that, while *autou* could refer back to *to soma*, "the body" (as it almost certainly does), it could also be taken to refer to Christ from verse 15, wherein one might ask again, "Does Christ need to be built up or made complete?" Essentially, the variant seems to demonstrate a split between the Alexandrian witnesses—those favoring the text on the one hand, and those that seem to stem from *Sinaiticus* on the other (excepting Codex *Bezae* [original corrector], a sixth-century Western witness). If one must choose, then, between *Sinaiticus*/*Bezae*, on the one hand, and the *Alexandrinus*/*Vaticanus*/Papyrus 46 combination on the other, the latter must prevail.

Christ's Purposes for His Church

Paul introduces here the theme of "gifts," adapting Psalm 68:18 (=Eph. 4:8) to his purpose.[3] In verses 9-10 he relates the earthly Jesus to the Christ who now reigns in heaven, "far above all rule and authority and power and dominion" (Eph. 1:21, *NASB*). This same Christ has given "gifts" to his Church: apostles, prophets, evangelists, pastors, and teachers.

Paul states the overall purpose of these gifts in verse 12, *pros ton katartismon ton hagion eis ergon diakonias, eis oikodomen tou somatos tou Cristou*. It is very important here to observe the interplay of the prepositions *pros* and *eis*. Many grammars scarcely recognize their use to express purpose or result, except when accompanied by a verb in the infinitive.[4] The generally preferred conception of *pros* with the accusative case is often simply "with reference to."[5] "Towards" is also generally accepted, though usually with strict qualifications. It is the idea of "towards" which tends, however, to imply an expression of purpose or expected result, *i.e.*, "moving towards" a result, especially when clearly outside of a local, spatial, or temporal context. C. F. D. Moule recognizes the possibility of "tending towards" or "leading to."[6] More specifically, he translates *pros oikodomen* in Romans 15:2 as "making for upbuilding," while Blass-Debrunner lists the same phrase (from Eph. 4:29) under "Purpose, result, destiny."[7]

Eis is treated similarly: it is recognized as occasionally expressing purpose or result, when used with the infinitive. But Dana-Mantey gives examples of such usage with an accusative case noun: *touto poieite eis ten emen anamnesin* (1 Cor. 11:24; *cf.* Mt. 8:4, 34; 2 Cor. 2:12).[8] Furthermore, Albrecht Oepke conceives the idea of "leading to," as in *eis zoen* (Mt. 7:14, 18:8f).[9]

While the general meanings of *pros* and *eis*, "with respect to" or "with reference to," could well be used here, it seems more likely in this context that purpose or result is intended. Paul's construction with both *pros* in verse 12, and *eis* in verses 12 and 13, is identical, but a substantial difference would seem probable.

The writer shall propose here that Paul has intended that *pros* express purpose, whereas *eis* is intended to denote an expected result. Therefore, the "gifts" have been provided *for the purpose of* the equipping of the saints, *with the expected results being* mutual service and the building up of the saints. This can probably be carried on through verse 13, since *mechri* ("until") is used conjunctively: what follows is "a punctiliarly conceived future event preceded in time by the action of the main clause."[10] Conceivably, this subordinates the rest of the passage through verse 16 under the originally expressed purpose, the *equipping* (*equipment*) of the saints. (All other purpose/result clauses in these verses are expressed with *eis* [as result] except for *pros ten methodeian tes planes*, which is descriptive of *nepioi* ["children"] and therefore incidental to the passage. In that case, further expected results of this equipping of the saints are *unity*, a *complete* (mature, perfect) *man*, and *the measure of the stature of the fullness of Christ*.[11] As far as can be determined here, these latter results come, in turn, as a result of the *work of service* and *the building up of the Body*.

Achieving the Stature of Christ

The assumption often made from superficial study of this passage is that each Christian is himself to grow up to match Christ in stature. Two attitudinal problems seem to stem from this line of reasoning: first, the germination of spiritual pride in those who come to feel they have achieved; second, an overburdening guilt that afflicts those who try, but continually fall short of that goal. Either way, the Christian who by his own strength reaches to fulfill the perfect standard sets himself up for a fall.

However, it is in the plural that this passage is addressed. It is the saints who are to be equipped; the Body that is to be built up; and "we" who are to attain unity and the stature of Christ, who are to be no longer children, etc. Again, it is the Body, not the part, which is to build itself up in love.

No individual can achieve the fullness of Christ himself. Christ has intended the Church to be his Body, and collectively to form the *mature man*, "for even as the body is one and yet has many members, and all the members of the body, though they are many, are one body, so also is Christ" (1 Cor. 12:12, *NASB*). To believe otherwise is to deny the sense of the passage, for it is centered upon the maturation and unification of the individual parts, thus bringing about the perfection of the whole.

The Nature of Christ's Fullness

Just as *fullness* is a general term in the English, so is *pleroma* in Greek. As Gerhard Delling remarks, ". . . in different passages several meanings or their totality may be implied."[12] It can carry various connotations, such as "that which fills, fullness, fulfilling, and is also used as an eschatological technical term for the fullness of time and the fulfillment of the will of God .[13]

The first issue that must be addressed is whether fullness here is used in the Gnostic sense. Some scholars, especially those who dispute the Pauline authorship of Ephesians, consider this usage to demonstrate an early form of that error. The term was, indeed, later used technically in Gnosticism to describe the spiritual realm which spans between man and God:

> Jesus brought the angels with Him from the pleroma, and they may not return thither without the gnostics. . . . The whole pleroma is the bridal chamber . . . into which enter the pneumatics who have put off their souls, found their angel bridegrooms, and become pure spirits . . . .[14]

This is hardly the teaching of Ephesians. While *pleroma* does occur in Ephesians 4:13, it could not be said to have a uniform meaning in all of its Pauline occurrences, or even elsewhere in Ephesians (1:10,23; 3:19). Delling notes that "The use in Col. follows a single line materially, but this differs from the three lines which are unquestionably to be found in Eph. both formally and in part materially."[15] R. M. Wilson goes further to suggest that the "later gnostic speculation" originated from Colossians 1:19, 2:9, and Ephesians 4:13, rather than the other way around.[16]

A more cogent theory is that, as Moule proposes, *fullness of Christ* is parallel to the preceding phrase, so that *mature man = fullness of Christ*.[17]   Indeed, it is not unlike Paul to say the same thing in two different ways as an emphatic device. However, grammatically the parallelism breaks down, since *man* is set parallel to *measure* (both in the accusative case), while *fullness of Christ* appears in the genitive. Yet the argument is strengthened if one considers *fullness* as descriptive of *stature* and translates thus: *the measure of the full stature that pertains to Christ* (*i.e.*, the measure [standard] of Christ = the mature [perfect] man).

Another possibility proposed herein is this: Paul has in essence drawn to-gether his thoughts upon the maturation of the Church into one phrase, expressing its perfection as the mature man. (One must observe that Paul's metaphors are mixed here—on the one hand the child/adult theme, on the other the unity-of-the-body theme.) The next phrase appears to be logically connected, though not full expressed: the measure of stature points back to the previous clause, while *tou pleromatos tou Christou* is descriptive of the nature of the One who is perfect in stature. This description is related to a recurrent theme throughout Ephesians, as well as Colossians: God has given Christ all authority and power (Eph. 1:20-23; *cf.* Col. 1:19, 2:9), which corresponds to *fullness*, for Christ "ascended far above all the heavens, that He might *fill all things*" (Eph. 4:10 [*NASB*], italics mine). As the Body of Christ, the Church is being filled (*pleroumenou*, Eph. 1:23; *plerothete*, Eph. 3:19; *cf. pepleromenoi*, Col 2:10) by the One who is already *full*. Christ does not have to be filled in any sense by the Church, for He already possesses Fullness—rather, the Church, by growing into the mature man, is to achieve the stature of Christ, which is characterized by Fullness in every way.

Conclusion

The merit of the foregoing argument is that it shows continuity in thought and theme throughout Ephesians and Colossians, and includes some of the most obscure and difficult themes and terminology. It has attempted to demonstrate such continuity, especially in the usage of fullness and filling—the former to express the all-encompassing authority and power of Christ given Him by the Father (as a state of being), the latter to express the engen-dering of completeness or perfection within the Church by means of providing Spirit-filled leadership, in the form of apostles, prophets, evangel-ists, pastors, and teachers. These leaders are for the equipping of the Church, and can do nothing more of themselves. Yet this preparation is to yield results, ultimately the maturation of the Body into the mature man—mature according to the measure of Christ. It is through Christ's own "Fullness" that He is able to perfect his Church, mature leadership being the instrument by which He "fills" it, thus accomplishing his goal.

Of course, one must take into account that "fullness" and "filling" are general terms, as easily used to refer to "being filled with the Spirit," the Scriptures "being fulfilled," "the fullness of time," the simple act of filling a vessel, etc. Whether any particular occurrence carries a specific, theologically loaded connotation, must be judged from the context.

The interpretation of Ephesians 4:7-16 proposed here certainly differs from many established interpretations, which in turn differ from one another. Yet, it has been successful if it provokes renewed consideration of the passage in the light of its claims. Perhaps it is, after all, through challenges to established modes of thought that "new" truth will be uncovered, or "old" truths strengthened.

NOTES

1. *Novum Testamentum Graece*, ed. Kurt Aland and Barbara Aland, et al., 26th ed. (Stuttgart: Deutsche Bibelstiftung, 1979).

2. The United Bible Societies, *The Greek New Testament*, ed. Kurt Aland et al., 3d ed. corrected (Stuttgart: Biblia-Druck GmbH., 1983).

3. *Cf.* T. K. Abbott, *A Critical and Exegetical Commentary on the Epistles to the Ephesians and Colossians*, ed. S. R. Driver, A. Plummer, and C. A. Briggs, *The International Critical Commentary* (Edinburgh: T. & T. Clark, 1897; rpt. ed. Edinburgh: T. & T. Clark, 1968), pp. 112. Abbott states, "The supposition that St. Paul does not intend either to quote exactly or to interpret, but in the familiar Jewish fashion adapts the passage to his own use, knowing that those of his readers who were familiar with the psalm would recognise the alteration and see the purpose of it, namely, that instead of receiving gifts of homage Christ gives his gifts to men, is not open to any serious objection, since he does not found any argument on the passage."

4. H. E. Dana and Julius R. Mantey, *A Manual Grammar of the Greek New Testament* (New York: Macmillan Publishing Co., 1955), pp. 104, 110. A. T. Robertson, *A Grammar of the Greek New Testament in the Light of Historical Research*, 5th ed. (New York: Harper and Bros. Publishers, 1923), p. 626.

5. F. Blass and A. Debrunner, *A Greek Grammar ol the New Testament and Other Early Christian Literature*, trans. and rev. Robert W. Funk (Chicago: The Univ. of Chicago Press, 1961), p. 124. Robertson, p. 626.

6. Charles F. D. Moule, *An Idiom Book of New Testament Greek*, 2d ed. (Cambridge, Eng.: At the University Press, 1971), p. 53.

7. Blass-Debrunner, p. 124.

8. Dana and Mantey, p. 104.

9. Albrecht Oepke. "*Eis*," in *Theological Dictionary of the New Testament*, ed. Gerhard Friedrich, trans. and ed. Geoffrey W. Bromiley (Grand Rapids: Wm. B. Eerdmans Publishing Co., 1968), 2:424.

10. Nigel Turner, "Syntax," *A Grammar of New Testament Greek*, vol. 3, by James H. Moulton (Edinburgh: T. & T. Clark, 1963), P. 111.

11. Note the exclusion of *eis auton* (v. 15), which expresses the result of *auxesomen*, and likewise *eis oikodomen*, the result of *poieitai*. On the other hand, *hina meketi omen nepioi* in itself expresses the purpose or result of the equipping of the saints.

12. Gerhard Delling, "*Pleres, pleroo, pleroma, anapleroo, antanapleroo, ekpleroo, ekplerosis, sumpleroo, plerophoreo, plerophoria*," in *Theological Dictionary of the New Testament*, ed. Gerhard Friedrich, trans. and ed. Geoffrey W. Bromiley (Grand Rapids: Wm. B. Eerdmans Publishing Co., 1968), 6:298.

13. Reinier Schippers, "Fullness, Abound, Multitude, Fulfil, Make Room," in *The New International Dictionary of New Testament Theology*, gen. ed. Colin Brown (Grand Rapids: Zondervan Publishing Co., 1975), 1:728.

14. Delling, p. 301.

15. Delling, p. 304.

16. R. M. Wilson, "Gnosis, Gnosticism and the New Testament," in U. Bianchi, ed., *Le Origini dello Gnosticism* (n.p., 1967), pp. 518ff., cited by Schippers, 740. See also Craig Evans, "The Colossian Mystics, *Biblica* 63 (1982):190-91.

17. Charles F. D. Moule, "'Fulness' and 'Fill' in the New Testament," *Scottish Journal of Theology* 4 (1951):81.

Chapter 22.   Fullness of Christ and Maturation of the Church

What Christ's Exaltation Means to the Church

Much recent theology swings too far toward the mystical aspects of Christ's work, to the neglect of the physical, here-and-now results which we see, or ought to see, taking place among us. If there is indeed a present, physical, concrete result of Christian faith, it is in the quarters in which evangelism is stressed—that others might believe and be saved. This is good, and appropriate to the purpose of the Church: but even this is ultimately mystical if the Christianizing process is allowed to end there, where an acknowledgement of the truth of the gospel, water baptism, the regular exercise of public worship, etc., are allowed to represent the acme of religious experience. Christianity, according to Scripture, is much more than simply believing and having one's salvation secure.

The Apostle Paul made this point quite clear: one can be Christian and saved, yet fall far short of Christ's standard and purpose. As Paul declares to the Corinthians,

> *I could not speak to you as spiritual men, but as carnal, like mere infants in Christ; I gave you milk, not solid food, for you could not stand it, nor yet are you able; you are still carnal, since jealousy and discord exist among you—are you not then carnal, and live according to man's ways?* (1 Cor 3:1-3).

Instead, the Christian is to become a spiritual man who "judges all things, but himself is judged by no one" (1 Cor 2:15) and corporately "a complete man, unto the measure of stature of the fullness of Christ, that we might no longer be children . . ." (Eph 4;13 f.).

The maturation theme runs consistently throughout the Pauline documents; but the maturation of the Christian does not begin with the teachings of man, not even of the great Apostle, but with Christ himself. As Paul explains, the perfection of each individual Christian flows directly from the throne of God, wherein Christ is seated—and is an end-product of Christ's Exaltation. This "fullness" of Christ, as Paul describes it, is manifested through Christ's gifts to men: gifts intended to serve the edification (which is more than mere encouragement and emotional uplifting) of the Church in this present world. Christ, in his omnipotence, bestows upon men the tools to make spiritual men of themselves and others.

Methodology

Some might object to the seemingly eclectic nature of this study, taking as it does scattered passages from various Bible books. However, the use of these passages does not, in the author's opinion, violate the overall context of the Pauline corpus or the immediate context of individual passages. The author presumes that the letters traditionally attributed to Paul are indeed Pauline. Modern theories to the contrary are just that—theories. Rather, comparing theology, here specifically christology and pneumatology, as well as termi-nology and metaphor, may establish Pauline authorship, especially within a sizeable corpus written over a period of some years to widely varied audi-ences. In such case, were the authorship not consistent, one would expect considerable theological and metaphorical inconsistency.

Verses pertinent to salient points have been listed afterward with little or no elaboration, for purposes of brevity. They have been included so that the reader may examine the scriptural evidence and draw his own conclusions.

The Meaning of Fullness

Pauline usage of the terms "fullness" (*pleroma*), "fill" or "fulfill" (*pleroun*), and "full" (*pleres*) varies widely. An extended exposition of possible mean-ings is not intended here; nevertheless, a concise list of generally-accepted meanings of the "filling" idea is appropriate:

1. Simple filling, as in filling a vessel. This includes the ideas of filling with joy (Phil 2:2, Rom 15:13), with the Holy Spirit (Eph 5:18), with knowledge (Rom 15:14, Col 1:9), with righteousness (Phil 1:11) or with unrighteousness (Rom 1:29).

2. Completing a pre-set quantity, especially of sins[1] (1 Th 2:16, *cf*. Mt 23:32, 2 Cor 10:6, Col 1:24, 2 Th 1:11; possibly also Rom 15:19).

3. Realizing a pre-determined event or condition, as in fulfill-ing Mosaic Law (Rom 8:4, 13:8, 10; Gal 5:14, 6:2), God's will (Col 1:25, 4:17; 2 Th 1:11; see also Acts 13:22), a pro-

phetic time (Rom 11:25, Gal 4:4, Eph 1:10) or a mission (Rom 15:19, Gal 4:17).

4. Satisfying needs or desires (Rom 15:24, 2 Cor 7:4, Eph 2:3, Phil 4:18, 2 Tim 1:4).

5. Expressing richness or completeness (Rom 11:12, 15:29; probably also Eph 1:23, 3:19, 4:10, 13; Col 1:19, 2:9; *cf.* Jn 1:16).[2]

6. Equivalent to or in special relationship with *ta panta*, "all things," signifying all creation or all powers of the universe (1 Cor 10:26, 28; possibly also Eph 1:22 f., Col 1:19 f., *cf.* Eph 1:9 f., 4:10).

7. As a sort of "Christianese," technical terminology already developing in the Christian Church.[3]

8. Allegedly as technical terminology drawn from Gnosticism, Stoicism, or some other outside source. This usually entails the more ambiguous passages: Eph 1:22 f., 3:19, 4:10, 13; Col 1:19, 2:9.

The latter classification is by far the most disputed. Scriptural ambiguity seems to breed not only dissent, but applications foreign to the context. Such has been the case in a number of modern theories of New Testament origins. Let us examine, by way of example, the results of the exegesis of such a disputed passage, presuming a technical use of terminology from non-Christian (or "extra-Christian") sources. As Elaine Pagels formulates a Gnostic interpretation and application of Ephesians 4:12b-16,

> Paul anticipates here that the pneumatic element (Christ and the elect) shall "unite in faith" (*cf.* 4:13) "elements that seem to be divided," that is, the psychic and the pneumatic. What is now woman (the psychic) shall be transformed to become man (pneumatic), joined with the man to constitute the "perfect man" who is Christ. The Valentinians explain that both psychics and pneumatics need to "grow," but the process of growth differs in each case. The pneumatic seed, sown in a state of infancy, grows continually, naturally, to maturity; the psychic must be transformed and changed from his slave status to that of adopted sonship. Both processes effect the

growth of the whole ecclesia into "one body" united and headed by Christ.[4]

While the unity theme here does not entirely violate the context, certain themes and ideas are quite alien to Paul. Nowhere in Paul (nor elsewhere in Scripture) does "woman" represent the soulish realm, and "man" the spiritual; nor is woman to become man. Further, it is the unity of all Christians (*hoi pantes*) and the knowledge of Christ which are to produce the "complete man" (v. 13), not the joining of soul to spirit.

Then the soulish state is to Paul the "natural man," (*psuchikos*, 1 Cor 2:14 f.). He does not relate this directly to slavery: slavery is to sin (Rom 6:6, 16, 17, 20) and to lust (Titus 3:3). Moreover, the subject addressed in this passage is not slavery, but maturation. This maturation is to come, ultimately, through Christ's gifts (Eph 4:7), administered by leaders, prophets, and teachers (v. 11), serving to equip, edify, unify, and educate all Christians (vv. 12-13). The result is not a higher cosmic state, as the Gnostics hoped to achieve, but a physically manifest improvement in comportment: that they might be resistant to false doctrine (v. 14) and practice greater love (vv. 15-16). This maturity produces the *fullness of Christ* in the Church as a whole. The individual does not achieve a mystical or cosmic "fullness" which makes him semi-divine and part of the *Pleroma*, as many Gnostics held, where he joins the angels and Christ who span between God and the world.

Such exegesis is the result of the imposition of external technical meanings and a pre-conceived theology upon a text.[5] In regard to the Gnostics, it is far more likely that they drew from Paul than the other way around.[6] That Paul did not use "fullness" consistently is self-evident. Even elsewhere in Ephesians (1:10), he writes *pleromatos tōn kairōn*, "fullness of times." The very least that can be said is that Paul usually used *pleroma* as other New Testament writers did: in a general way, not necessarily loading it with theological meaning apart from the immediate context.

This is not to say that there is no technical terminology in the New Testament. The New Testament writers were using the Greek language, often to express Jewish and Christian ideas that were themselves foreign to the Greek idiom. There is a degree of technical sense in such a construction as *fullness of time*, in which the Jew or Christian could derive a greater, or at least more distinct, meaning than a pagan Greek who was ignorant of Scripture.

With this in mind, one might conceive that with *pleroma* Paul was using a sort of "Christianese," which was beginning to spring up, and even that he coined it as a theological term himself. After all, how could one describe the omnipotence, self-sufficiency and universal dominion of God, if not by *fullness*? And how else could one sum up the position of Christ, to whom all God's authority was committed, except by *fullness*? Paul, who used the same word in so many other senses, could then apply it to that which is ineffable in its incomprehensibility—just as "Almighty" so miserably fails to run the gamut of God's nature, yet in its stark simplicity seems to express that very thought. One might well imagine Paul, rambling on in his discursive style, pausing at the point when he must express this total Exaltation of Christ, and choosing the simple but eloquent and verbally potent *fullness*.

The Exaltation (Fullness) of Christ

Nowhere is the Exaltation of Christ presented more clearly than in Ephesians. In chapter 1, all things are consummated in Christ (v. 10), and God has seated Christ at his right hand (v. 20). He is placed above all rulers and authorities both of earth and of eternity (v. 22). In chapter 4, Christ is He who *descended* to the earth so that He might again *ascend*, in order to *fill all things* (v. 10). Through Christ's gifts, the Church is to achieve unity and knowledge—becoming, metaphorically, a *mature* (perfect, complete) *man* (v. 13). This mature man is to be equal in stature to Christ himself, thus representing his *fullness*.[7]

Moreover, this theme is not absent elsewhere in Paul. In Romans, Christ has been freed from the dominion of death, and now lives unto God (6:4-10). He now is seated on God's right hand, interceding for his own (8:34). In First Corinthians, Christ has been made the foundation of his Church (3:11). Christians have been made the possession of Christ and subject to him, as He is subject to God (3:23, *cf.* 11:3). In time, Christ will abolish all other powers, subjecting them all unto himself, then turning them over to God the Father (15:24-28). In Philippians, God has exalted Christ, and given him a name at which every being, whether earthly or heavenly, must kneel (2:9-11). Christ will one day transform the bodies of his saints to a higher state, by exerting the power of his authority (3:21). In Colossians (so similar in content and theology to Ephesians that some have thought one to be a forgery of the other), all Creation has been made *by* and *for* Christ. He is supreme, and is head of the Church, since God chose to embody in Christ all *fullness* (1:16-19).[8] Man should avoid falling prey to human wisdom, since it is in Christ that the fullness of deity dwells, Christ being the head of all rulership and authority (2:9-10).[9] Once again, in 3:1, Christ is seated at the right hand of God.

The Exaltation theme remains consistent throughout Paul. Christ is not a dead hero, or merely a prophet or teacher of righteousness. Christ is alive and well and seated in the throne of God. There He continues to work in power for his Church—in fact, does a far more effectual work than He could perform within the physical limitations of a human body. Although subordinate to God, the Father has bestowed upon Christ authority over all things so that only the Father himself is excepted. God's purpose is to fulfill through Christ his eternal purpose, the redemption of men and defeat of Satan. Christ will, in the end, take the Church up to himself as his bride.

These teachings of Paul continue the teachings of the Gospel itself, for Christ declared his period of witness, his death and resurrection, his ascent to the throne of God, and his bestowal of gifts through the Baptism in the Holy Spirit, in order to equip and enable his Church.

Paul's Head/Body Metaphors

The head/body metaphors found in the Pauline documents are illustrative of the relationship of Christ to the Church, and Christians to one another. Often these metaphors are taken as being more mystical than they actually are. The head/body relationship could be considered typological, in the sense of expressing correspondence: the head is to the body as Christ is to the Church. Such correspondence is key, for example, to the identification of Moses as a *type* of Christ: Moses was the intercessor between God and Israel in the same way that Christ intercedes for the Church.

Yet there is no reason to over-spiritualize Paul's illustration. He makes great use, elsewhere, of the metaphor of the Christian as a runner in a race, an athlete who must train and strive to win. But beyond vivid illustration, he places no great weight upon it. The metaphors of head and body, in turn, conjure up mental pictures which promote understanding. Generally, one is well advised to take them to be fulfilling their simple, contextual purpose, and not assume that *head* and *body* have in themselves theological import.

Head/body metaphors occur in Romans, First Corinthians, Ephesians, and Colossians. Of these occurrences, two can be eliminated from consideration: 1 Corinthians 11:3 and Colossians 2:10 are not relevant because they do not actually compare a head/body relationship to another corresponding relationship. 1 Corinthians 11:3 expresses the headship of Christ over man, and in turn the headship of God over Christ. Colossians 2:10 conveys the headship of Christ over all rule and authority. Both of them utilize *kephale*, "head," as equivalent to *arche*, "ruler."[10] Their themes support the premises of this study but are not germane to the present argument. Rather, we are concerned with the use of the head-to-body relationship in Paul to illustrate Christ's relationship to his Church.

The basic content of the metaphorical passages is broken down in Table 1. The methodology used here is as follows: An idea that is explicit or clearly implicit to the verse or passage is marked *YES*. Other ideas which appear possible or debatable rate a question mark. All other columns are left blank.

For example, in Romans 12:4-5, the term *body* is used in two, possibly three, senses. The most outstanding sense is simply metaphorical: just as the human body has many parts with diverse functions, so does the Church. Although *ekklesia*, "church," does not appear here, it is clearly implicit in "one body in Christ." The second sense is that of the Body as the assembly of believers. Third, it is possible to extend this sense to refer to that of "*the* Body of Christ," which in itself may have theological implications—though whether it is to be considered mystical or merely phraseological (in which case it is synonymous with *ekklesia*) is not of immediate concern here.[11]

	Christ as Head =*arche*	Christ as Head of the Church	Christ as Head of the Body	Church as Body (i.e., Group)	Church as "The Body of Christ"	Simple Metaphorical Comparison
Rom 12:4-5				YES	?	YES
1 Cor 12:12-27			?	YES	YES	YES
Eph 1:22-23	?	YES		?		?
Eph 4:4-16	?		?	?	?	YES
Eph 5:22-33	?	YES	?	?		YES
Col 1:18	?	YES	?	?	?	YES
Col 1:24			?	YES	YES	
Col 2:19	?		YES	?	?	YES
Col 3:15				YES	?	

Table 1
Basic Content of Pauline Head/Body Metaphors

What implications can be drawn? In as many as five cases, Christ is referred to as the authoritative *head* (if *kephale* is taken as equivalent to *arche*).[12] Three times, He is specifically called the head of the Church, at other times possibly designated the head of the Body (as the gathering of believers). In every passage, with the possible exception of Colossians 2:19, the object of the metaphor is expressly or implicitly identified as the Church or the assembled Body. The exception differs only in its lack of explicit identifications with Christ and the Church, but clearly echoes the thought of the other head/body passages. Interestingly, in every case in which the subject of the metaphor is given (which technically excludes Ephesians 4:4 and Colossians 3:15), it is God (Rom 12:4-5), both God and the Holy Spirit (1 Cor 12:12-27), or Christ. Thus the subject is always, in every mention, a member of the Trinity.[13] The significance here is that the metaphors are so close as to suggest homogeneity, at the very least.[14]

Of the head/body passages, only seven are in themselves complete metaphors, containing both subject and object. One can well conjecture that Paul assumed that his readers would understand the relationship he had in mind. Still it proves inconclusive whether and in which cases Paul indeed wrote *kephale* meaning *arche*, or *soma* meaning *ekklesia*.[15]

One can divide these remaining seven passages into three basic categories, as in Table 2. In the first, the Church is pictured as a physical body with many parts, each of which performs a different function. In the second, the Church is a body with Christ as its authoritative or functional Head. Third, the Church is a part of Christ's body in the same way that a wife's body is considered to be part of her husband's.[16] Ephesians 4:4-16 and Colossians 2:19 contain elements of each of the first two categories, while Ephesians 1:22-23 and Ephesians 5:22-33 span both the second and third.

The Church as Body with Diverse Parts & Functions	The Church as Body with Christ as the Head	The Church as Part of Christ as a Wife is Part of Her Husband
Rom 12:4-5		
1 Cor 12:12-27		(1 Cor 11:3)
	Eph 1:22-23	
Eph 4:4-16	Eph 5:22-33	
	Col 1:18	
	(Col 2:10)	
Col 2:19		

Table 2
Delineation of Paul's Head/Body Passages

It might seem, superficially, that these three respective categories of metaphorical comparison originated from as many different sources. However, proceeding from the assumption that all were written by Paul, and viewing them in the context of Paul's overall methodology, style, thought, and concerns, a consistent progression of thought can be demonstrated as follows:

Christ, as the *arche* of Creation, of all rule and authority, and of the Church, is the authoritative and functional "head"—the leader, master, and controller of the "body" (column 2). As exalted Lord and ruler of the Church, Christ has joined it unto himself. He maintains perfect beneficence toward the Church, as a husband should his wife, wishing to nourish, cherish, and protect it (column 3). He is able, as the authority over the body, and as the power of the universe, to provide for his Church in all things according to its needs (column 2). He accomplishes this by providing "gifts" to the Church, spiritually bestowed but materially manifested among the individual believers. These gifts are diversely distributed, and serve to complement one another, as the various parts of a physical body cooperate to serve the whole (column 1).

This progression demonstrates significant continuity in the thought of Paul and between elements of his theology which otherwise, as individual entities, might seem disjointed. Following this formulation, the giftedness of the Church is a direct result of the Exaltation (*fullness*) of Christ.

Christ Giving of Gifts to His Church

The purpose here is not to detail the various gifts themselves, as far as their definition and specific functions are concerned. There are plenty of other works on that subject. Rather, it is upon the *giving* of the gifts and upon the nature of the result of this giving that this discussion will focus.

Ephesians 4:4-16 demonstrates most vividly the progression from *fullness* to gifts. First, Paul uses Psalm 68:18 to illustrate the dispensation of gifts by virtue of Christ's exalted position (v. 8).[17] Then, parenthetically, he relates the Christ who ascended up into heaven, where He now "fills all things," to the man who had first "descended into the lower parts of the earth," namely, Jesus of Nazareth (vv. 9, 10). Paul lists the gifts which were given: apostles, prophets, evangelists, pastors, and teachers (v. 11).[18] He immediately states the purpose of these gifts: "the equipping of the saints for the work of service," and the edification of the Body (v. 12).[19] In v. 13, introduced by *mechri*, "until," Paul states the end product (or completion) of this process of edification: the *unity of the faith*, the *knowledge of the Son* and, finally, a *complete man* whose stature somehow equals that of Christ.[20] Then, vv. 14 ff. give the reasons for this edification (*hina*, "in order that"): that we might no longer be babes, might speak the truth in love, etc.

Elsewhere in Paul, this giving process, while hardly so comprehensive in detail, nevertheless continues to emerge in various forms. 1 Corinthians 12:28 parallels Ephesians 4:11, but after listing apostles, prophets, and teachers, lapses into specific manifestations: miracles, gifts of healings, helps, administrations, tongues. A number of other such *charismata* are listed in

12:8-10. The administration of these gifts is the same as in Ephesians (4:7), bestowed according to the divine will (1 Cor 12:11, 24; *cf.* Rom 12:3-8). There are various gifts, ministries, and workings (1 Cor 12:4-6), but one abiding purpose: the edification of the Church (1 Cor 12:7, 25; 14:3 f., 31; *cf.* 2 Cor 12:12, 19; Eph 4:12; Col 2:1-3, 3:12-17). In Romans 12:3-8, the gifts are prophecy, service, exhortation, giving, leadership, and beneficence, each to be practiced according to the measure by which God has allotted them. The Corinthians are said to abound in faith, word, knowledge, earnestness, and love (2 Cor 8:7). To the Ephesians (3:14-19), Paul expresses his hope that they might be strengthened and enlightened by the Spirit, even to be "filled to all the fullness of God" (see also 1:16-19). Similarly, he prays that the Colossians "might be filled with the knowledge of his will in all wisdom and spiritual understanding," to be spiritually strengthened, and to bear the fruit of steadfastness, patience, and thanksgiving (1:9-11). It is the Spirit of the Lord which has taken away the veil from Scripture, and now enables man to glimpse the glory of the Lord, as in a mirror (2 Cor 3:17 f.; *cf.* 1 Cor 13:12). Timothy is exhorted not to neglect the spiritual gift that is allotted to him (1 Tim 1:6, 18; 4:14). Paul speaks frequently of the fruit which the Spirit engenders (see Gal 5:22 f., Eph 5:9, Phil 1:11, Col 1:6, 2 Tim 2:22). In Romans 8, following the Spirit enables one to turn from the carnal unto the righteousness of God, as in Galatians 5:16 ff. The Holy Spirit, through the gifts, provides the link between man and God, and makes possible a godly life.

Still, the instrumental relationship between God, Christ, and the Spirit is not explicit in Paul. When referring to the origin of the gifts, Paul interchanges "from God," "from Jesus Christ," and "by the Spirit." Perhaps the blanks can best be filled in by looking through the eyes of other New Testament writers.

In the Gospel of John, beginning in the thirteenth chapter, Jesus addresses his disciples concerning events in the near future. He would soon be leaving them, He announced. But He would not leave them without comfort and guidance. He would send his disciples another Paraclete, the Holy Spirit, to abide with them, teaching them all things and bringing his words to remembrance (14:16, 26; 15:26). The spirit would enable them to excel even the incarnate Christ, doing "greater works" by virtue of Christ's new position of Exaltation (14:12-14, 15:7, 16).21 It is expedient that Christ ascend to the Father's throne, rather than remain—for only then can He send forth the Spirit (16:7 f.). Yet the Spirit will not glorify himself, but will testify of Christ, and transmit to them his message (15:26, 16:13-15).

In John, then, the power is God's, the authority and message is Christ's, and the medium of transmission is the Holy Spirit. The Spirit is sent to dwell with and in them (14:17, 20, 23). In this way they are "gifted"—although John does not use the term—being empowered to do miraculous things, the work of Christ, as his agents.

Again, in the Acts, Luke (?) declares the promise of the Holy Spirit to empower the disciples (1:4-8). This was made manifest in the miracle of tongues in Acts 2, and throughout the book in the many instances of prophecy, tongues, healing foreknowledge, and other miraculous events. In Acts, the declaration of God through Christ is always the message, but the Spirit is the medium.

Neither of these accounts violate, but rather confirm and complement the Pauline teachings. To Paul, "God has sent forth the Spirit of the Son," by which the Christian is acknowledged as a child of God (Gal 4:6, cf. Rom 8:14-16, 1Th 4:8). The Christian knows God only through the Spirit (1 Cor 3:16, 6:19; see also Rom 8:9, 11; Eph 2:22). The Spirit gives comfort, witnessing to the Christian of his security in adoption (Rom 8:15 f., Gal 4:5 f.), making intercession beyond the limits of human comprehension (Rom 8:26 f.; cf. 1 Cor 14:14), engendering hope (Gal 5:5; cf. Rom 8:23-25, 1 Cor 14:31), as well as love among the saints (Col 1:8), and abiding in grace together with the human spirit (2 Tim 4:22, Philemon 25). The Spirit is the earnest of that which is to come, by which the believer is sealed until the day of final redemption (2 Cor 1:22, 5:5; Eph 1:13 f., cf. 1 Cor 12:13). Through him man is sanctified and justified before God (1 Cor 6:11, 2 Th 2:13), and continually changed into the image of Christ (2 Cor 3:18, Eph 4:13, 15). The Spirit provides access to God (Eph 2:18), distributes charismatic gifts (1 Cor 12:11), physically manifests the things of God (1 Cor 12:7), performs signs and miracles through men (Rom 15:19, 1 Cor 2:4), reveals the hidden things of God (1 Cor 2:10, Eph 3:5, 1 Tim 4:1; see also 1 Cor 14:31), guides the individual (Rom 8:14, 1 Cor 7:40, Gal 1:17 f., 5:18), unifies the Body (Eph 4:3 f., 13; cf. Phil 2:1-4), strengthens (Eph 3:16, Col 1:11), and acts as a medium for spiritual worship (1 Cor 14:14-17, Phil 3:3).

The Maturation of the Church

Christ has not bestowed his gifts indiscriminately or without purpose. In the twelfth and fourteenth chapters of First Corinthians, it is the lack of structure and control, which was producing confusion, plus a hedonistic preoccupation with the gifts that precluded true charismatic ministry in unity and love, for which Paul chides the Corinthians. But Christ had ordained neither confusion nor hyper-individualism in the Church. Instead, He gifted men to hold positions of leadership and service. These men were not necessarily chosen for their own natural abilities or aptitudes, but were to be endued with spiritual power. In spite of Paul's natural zeal and energy, he confessed, "I will glory in my weaknesses, that the power of Christ might rest upon me . . . for when I am weak, then I am mighty!" (2 Cor 12:9, 10; *cf.* 1 Cor 15:10). "You have not chosen me," Jesus pronounced, "but I have chosen you and appointed you that you might go forth and bear fruit . . ." (Jn 15:16; *cf.* Acts 9:15 f.). Again, Paul writes,

> *You see your calling, brothers, that there are not many wise according to the flesh, not many powerful, not many noble; but God chose the foolish things of the world to shame the wise, and the weak things of the world God chose to shame the strong, the base and contemptible things of the world God has chosen: the things that are not, to negate the things which are, that no mortal may boast before God* (1 Cor 1:26-29; *cf.* 2 Tim 1:9).

It is the empowerment of the Spirit, to Paul "the grace that is given me" (see Rom 12:3, 6, 15:15; 1 Cor 1:4-5, 3:10; 2 Cor 8:7; Eph 3:2, 7, 8; 2 Th 2:16-17) which is able to span the chasm of human frailty.

While it appears that many who were gifted were to serve more as helps to the congregation than as leaders, many others clearly were to administer God's authority over the Body in positions of leadership and education. According to Paul, the apostles and prophets are the foundation of the Church (Eph 2:20). He himself has received his commission from God (Col 1:25; *cf.* 2 Cor 10:13), according to Christ's own purposes (2 Tim 1:9), confirmed by such miracles as were expected of apostleship (2 Cor 12:12; *cf.* Rom 15:19, 1 Cor 2:4). Such authority is given for the edification of the Church, for building up and not tearing down (2 Cor 10:8, 13:10). The work of the apostles, prophets, evangelists, pastors, and teachers is ultimately to yield the *complete man*, the Church attaining the very stature of Christ (Eph 4:11-16; *cf.* 2 Cor 10:8, 12:19).

Moreover, those in leadership are to be "nourished by the words of faith and sound teaching" (1 Tim 4:6). The chief authorities, in turn, are to delegate authority to others who are of sound character, faithful, and learned in the things of God, able to teach others (2 Tim 2:2, Titus 1:5, 9).[22] Elders who are gifted in both preaching and teaching are worthy of double honor (1 Tim 5:17), Paul himself being appointed as preacher and teacher, as well as apostle (2 Tim 1:11). Such leaders are to work in others the same spiritual fruit that they have received by grace (2 Cor 8:6 f., 2 Tim 2:1 f.; see also Eph 4:29; Phil 1:7, 5:17; 1 Th 1:6).

The maturation passages in Paul, like the Christ/Church ("head"/"body") passages, are rich in metaphor. These metaphors fall into four basic categories:

1. *Those that compare the Church or the individual Christian to a building.* The Church is built upon Christ, the cornerstone, by gifted men, to become the temple of God (1 Cor 3:9-17, Eph 2:19-22).

2. *Those that compare the Church to a well-ordered physical body with Christ as the head.* The parts of the body are intended to complement one another in function (1 Cor 2:12-27), nourish one another (Col 2:19), and cooperate as an entity to edify the whole (Eph 4:15-16).

3. *One that describes the ideal Church as a mature man.* In Ephesians 4:11-15, the Church, through its self-edification, is to "grow up" to equal the stature of Christ (*cf.* 1 Cor 3:1-3).

4. *Those that consider the Church to be changing into the image of Christ.* In Romans 8:28-34, the Church is being changed[23] according to the eternal plan of God, through the exalted position of Christ, that Christ might become "firstborn of many brethren" (v. 29). In 2 Corinthians 3:18, the Spirit having opened men's eyes to the truth of God, they are then changed "from glory to glory."[24] The *new man* in Colossians 3:10 is "being renewed (*anakainoumenos*) unto knowledge according to the image of him who created him."

A fifth category that could be included involves Paul's "old man"/"new man" terminology (see Rom 6:4-23; 2 Cor 5:14-21; Gal 6:14-16; Eph 2:13-18, 4:20-25; Col 3:1-17). However, the "new man" idea is not that of a maturing Church. In Paul, the *new man*, if not purely metaphorical, is mystically created in the individual at the point of the salvation experience. The *old man* is buried with Christ, the *new man* raised with him. This *new man*, being already dead (2 Cor 5:14, Col 3:3), is free from bondage to sin (Rom 6:9, 22; Gal 6:14). The fact of sinfulness remains, but he is henceforth called to "put away the former manner of life" (Eph 4:22; *cf.* Rom 6:12, Col 3:5) and "put on" the fruit befitting God's elect (Col 3:12-14; see also Rom 6:13, Eph 4:24).[25]

Elsewhere in Paul, the Church's maturation process is described in more concrete terms. Paul gave pertinent instructions to Timothy and Titus concerning their personal conduct and the appointment of elders (1 Tim 3:1-13, 4:6 ff.; 2 Tim 2:2, 3:14-4:5; Titus 1:5-9). The leaders of the churches were to epitomize Christian conduct, teaching by good example (see 1 Cor 4:16, 11:1; Phil 3:17; 1 Th 1:6; 1 Tim 3:7, 4:12; Titus 2:8, 10), as well as by scholarship (Eph 4:11-13; 1 Tim 1:13, 4:6, 16; 2 Tim 2:15, 4:2; Titus 1:9, 2:7). In turn, the members of the Church were to work to edify and teach one another (Rom 12:1-21, 14:19, 15:2; 1 Cor 10:23 f., 12:25, 14:12; Eph 4:29; Phil 2:1-4; Col 3:12-17; Titus 2:4 f.). Through these efforts, the Christians were to mature personally and/or corporately (Rom 1:12, 12:2, 15:13-16; 1 Cor 1:4-7; Eph 4:12; Phil 1:6, 9-11; Col 1:9-12, 3:12-14; 1 Th 3:9-4:12; see also 2 Cor 7:1), until achieving a state of completion or "perfectness" (Eph 3:14-19, 4:13; Col 1:28, 4:12; 2 Tim 3:17; see also 2 Cor 13:9, 11; Gal 3:3).

By this long process the fullness of Christ has come full circle, being made manifest among his saints by their actions, lifestyle, outlook, mutual love and forbearance, and mature spiritual walk. Christ has indeed made for himself a people, and for his glory.

Summary

If judged successful, this study accomplishes the following: (1) deals with many of the problem passages in Paul, placing them squarely in his theology; (2) illustrates the need to interpret terminology according to its context by demonstrating variance in usage within the same thought system; (3) minimizes the need for a technical sense to such terms as *fullness* and *body*, showing instead general or multiple senses; (4) shows clear, concrete meanings behind superficially obscure metaphors; (5) demonstrates a horizontal thought continuum throughout the Pauline letters as well as some non-Pauline parallels; and 6) demonstrates a vertical continuum from the Exaltation (*fullness*) passages through the Church maturation passages.

Most of all, however, this study shows that there is a particular reason for Christ's *fullness*: Never does Paul say that men are saved by the Exaltation of Christ. Men are saved by belief in his atoning death and resurrection; but through Christ's Exaltation to the throne of God, He is able to bestow upon the Church the gifts necessary to make it the true instrument of ministry He has ordained it to become.

Notes

1. This idea of fulfilling a set quantity of sins may have been garnered from the Old Testament (see Gen 15:16, Dan 8:23), and developed more extensively during the Inter-Testamental Period (see 2 Maccabees 6:14, Wisdom 19:3 ff.; *cf.* 2 Esdras 7:76 f.).

2. According to Van Roon, "To the Hellenistic Jew, the words *pleres, pleroun,* and *empimplanai* in any event conveyed the association of salvation or blessedness," A. Van Roon, *The Authenticity of Ephesians* (Leiden: E. J. Brill, 1974), p. 229.

3. This would more or less presume, but does not necessarily demand, a late dating of the document, since such usage takes time to evolve.

4. Elaine H. Pagels, *The Gnostic Paul: Gnostic Exegesis of the Pauline Letters* (Phila.: Fortress Press, 1975), p. 123.

5. Other theories that prior or divergent theology appears in Paul could be treated to similar effect, demonstrating that Paul is not saying what they make him out to say. Of course, some terminology might have been borrowed or adapted to Paul's purpose. Stoicism, for example, originating three centuries before Paul, and prolific in Greek ideology, no doubt produced generally-accepted terms and ideas that crept into common Greek idiom and vocabulary, as did more ancient mythologies. Greek terms and idiom, moreover, were the tools with which Paul must necessarily build. On Stoic influence on Paul's theology, see Ernst Käseman, *Perspectives on Paul* (Phila.: Fortress Press, 1971), pp. 103-4. Roels considers that influence upon Paul's theology was far more Jewish than Hellenistic, Edwin D. Roels, *God's Mission: The Epistle to the Ephesians in Mission Perspective* (Amsterdam: Vrije Universiteit te Amsterdam, 1962), p. 87.

6. See Roels, *God's Mission*, p. 86 f., and Reinier Shippers, *"Pleroo,"* in *The New International Dictionary of New Testament Theology*, ed. Colin Brown, 3 vols. (Grand Rapids: Zondervan Publishing House, 1975), p. 740.

7. The phrase in Ephesians 4:13, *eis metron helikias tou pleromatos ton Christon,* is one of many ambiguous compound genitives in Paul. This construction could perhaps most clearly be rendered, "unto the measure of stature (*i.e.,* full height) which pertains to Christ, which is characterized by fullness" (*i.e.,* "richness," "completeness," as in item 5 of the list of possible meanings). This reading effectively defuses the mystery of the passage by rendering *fullness* as descriptive of Christ, rather than as a pagan technical term, or as some obscure theological "open sesame."

8. *Fullness* here may connote richness or completeness as before; or, since the Creation theme permeates this passage, the "fullness" that dwells in Christ may be a parallel to Creation (=*ta panta*), which has been subjected to him. Still, a third possibility, quite in context, is that God has transferred his own utter su-

premacy ("fullness") to Christ, giving him first place (v. 18). The latter seems most cogent in the light of 2:9, 10.

9. In 2:10, Christians are *fulfilled* (*pepleromenoi*) by virtue of the *fullness* of deity which dwells in Christ (*cf.* Eph 3:19). Since these are both general terms, it cannot readily be assumed that Paul intends a word-play, *i.e.*, an exceptional relationship between the two. However, the thought seems very close to Ephesians 4:13 in which, through the use of Christ's gifts, the Church is to be matured to the stature of the fullness of Christ. In the one, then, Christians are *fulfilled* to Christ's *fullness*; in the latter, they are *matured* to Christ's *maturity*.

10. *Contr.* George Howard, "The Head/Body Metaphors of Ephesians," *New Testament Studies* 20 (April 1974):352 f.

11. In such cases, the passages marked "YES" on the table designate the simple occurrence of the appellation *body of Christ* without a contextual hint of its exact meaning.

12. Grammatically, it is in unclear, in Ephesians 1:22, whether Christ is head over *all things* (=Creation? rule and authorities?), or the Church, or both.

13. Romans 12:4-5, for example, is prefaced by "God has allotted to each a measure of faith" (v. 3). Then, 1 Corinthians 12 speaks of gifts flowing to the Body *through* the Holy Spirit, as well as referring to "God who works all things in all" (v. 6). While Paul often seems to refer to Christ by the generic use of "God," he might actually be viewing God as being the ultimate source above and beyond Christ. Then the Holy Spirit is the instrument through which the will of God and Christ is accomplished.

14. Colossians 1:24, however, simply makes reference to the Church as Christ's body while dealing with another subject. The question remains whether *Church* and *Body* refer to the universal Church, or merely to the individual assembly.

15. Roels comments that the emphasis in Ephesians 1:22 is not upon Christ's headship, but that "all the power and the glory which are Christ's will be used to serve the interests of the church, which is his body," Roels, *God's Mission*, p. 105.

16. The idea of the body joined to Christ is also expressed in 1 Corinthians 6:15-17. However, this clearly refers to the individual Christian, not to the Church as a whole.

17. A cogent and concise explanation of Paul's apparent mishandling of this quotation comes from T. K. Abbott, *A Critical and Exegetical Commentary on the Epistles to the Ephesians and Colossians*, in The International Critical Commentary, vol. 35, ed. S. R. Driver, A. Plummer, and C. A. Briggs (Edinburgh: T. & T. Clark, 1897; rpt. ed. Edinburgh: T. & T. Clark, 1968), p. 112. He states, "The

supposition that St. Paul does not intend either to quote exactly or to interpret, but in the familiar Jewish fashion adapts the passage to his own use, knowing that those of his readers who were familiar with the psalm would recognise the alteration and see the purpose of it, namely, that instead of receiving gifts of homage Christ gives His gifts to men, is not open to any serious objection, since he does not found any argument on the passage." This says much about Paul's method of illustration. If the passage is thus considered as merely illustrative of the verses that follow it, the seeming mystery of the whole discussion is effectively mitigated.

18. Here it seems that the "gifts" were men, equipped to fulfill the offices God deemed necessary, rather than the offices themselves. As Abbott (p. 117) states, "It is not merely the fact of the institution of the offices that [Paul] wishes to bring into view, but the fact that they were gifts to the Church. Christ gave the persons; the Church appointed to the office." *Cf.* Roels, p. 185.

19. The text reads, *pros ton katartismon . . . eis ergon diakonias eis oikodomen.*" It is likely that "equipping," preceded by *pros*, is the expressed purpose, while "work of service" and "edification" (with *eis*) are the expected results. It is unclear, however, whether the two *eis* clauses should be connected with an assumed *kai*, or whether *eis oikodomen* is subordinate, *i.e.*, equipping → work of service → edification.

20. "Unity" and "knowledge," each introduced by *eis* and coordinated by *kai*, appear to be parallel. However, the "perfect (complete) man" clause, not coordinated by *kai*, appears to be a further result. Moule admits, "Here it seems most natural to take the closing phrase as parallel to and virtually identical in meaning with the preceding phrase, 'a fullgrown man'; so that 'the measure of the stature of the fulness of Christ' may mean 'the full height (in the metaphorical sense, of course, of *spiritual* maturity) represented by Christ's completeness.'" Charles F. D. Moule, "'Fulness' and 'Fill' in the New Testament," *Scottish Journal of Theology* 4 (1951):81. However, Moule considers it extreme optimism to think that man could attain Christ's own stature. But since the entire passage is plural (*hoi pantes*, v. 13; *nepioi*, v. 14, etc.), and the overall context is corporate, it is properly the entire Church which is mystically (?) to grow up into Christ (*cf.* Roels, pp. 204-5).

21. In John, by this juncture Christ has already declared himself to be glorified by the Father, having all the power of God at his disposal (13:3, 31, 16:15).

22. *Cf.* Hebrews 5:12. The writer of Hebrews, like Paul in 1 Corinthians 3:1-2, considers the church members to be infants who cannot take solid food, and therefore require milk. He considers that, by that time, they should not only have grown beyond elementary teachings and exhortations, but should have themselves become teachers of others.

23. It is uncertain, grammatically, whether the conforming to Christ's image here is punctiliar—occurring mystically at salvation—or a continuous process occurring thereafter. While one would expect to find some implication in a verb form, "conformed" is instead the adjective *summorphos*, "together-formed." Moreover, nothing germane to this question can be drawn from the immediate context.

24. The present-tense verb *metamorphoumai* cannot by itself be said with certainty to indicate a progressive sense, but continuous action is implied by "from glory to glory." *Cf.* Alfred Plummer, *A Critical and Exegetical Commentary on the Second Epistle of St. Paul to the Corinthians*, in The International Critical Commentary on the Holy Scriptures of the Old and New Testaments, vol. 34, pp. 106, 107.

25. A slight exception in gist occurs in Ephesians 2:13-18, in which the "new man" appears to refer to the Church as a whole being united with Christ to form a new, metaphorical man, rather than the regenerated individual becoming himself a new man.

Chapter 23.   Toward a Theology of the Exaltation of Christ

A Proposal for Further Study

In a review of Dr. Delmer Guynes' book, *The Gospel of the Ascension* (see Appendices), I asserted that the doctrines of the Ascension and Exaltation of Christ were central to Pentecostal theology, and "should rank alongside the Incarnation and the Atonement."[1] Put briefly, God performed these works in and through Jesus, they are essential to the very nature and existence of the Church, and they provide for the dispensation of spiritual gifts throughout the Church Age.

Jesus' Ascension and his Exaltation to the right hand of the throne of God were divine works of meaning and power beyond human comprehension. Yet, we can and should derive great meaning, truth, and application from these acts, as we do from the Incarnation, Atonement, Transfiguration, etc. Not only are the works of Christ in his Exaltation important in themselves, but they have direct bearing upon such Pentecostal distinctives as the Baptism in the Holy Spirit, spiritual gifts, and divine healing.   With a view toward the refinement and expansion of Pentecostal theology, I would like to delineate the subject while proposing areas for further study.

Where Ascension Ends and Exaltation Begins

How are the Ascension and the Exaltation to be delineated? In common usage, the terms seem synonymous. But "ascension" is obviously the act of ascending, and "exaltation" the act of exalting oneself or being exalted. While the meanings might overlap, they are not synonymous.

Practically and, I think, Biblically speaking, the Ascension is the act or process of Jesus acquiring his glorified body, receiving all the power and authority given him by the Father, and realizing in every other way the state of continuing exaltation that was always his birthright. In other words, the Ascension is to be thought of as the act of Jesus acceding to his Exaltation. I posit the Ascension not as an act distinct from or preliminary to the Exaltation but as an initiatory or activating phase. Moreover, the Exaltation can be considered an ongoing process even today, in that not yet have all things been put under Christ's feet,[2] and He is to be still more glorified in end-time events.[3]

Many details remain a mystery. When does the Ascension begin and end? Does it begin with his atoning death on the cross, or even earlier; or with his resurrection from the tomb? Some count the purported visit of Jesus to hell during his interment as an Ascension event.[4] But after the Resurrection, Jesus seems to announce a yet forthcoming Ascension to Mary in the garden,

> Do not keep clinging to me; I have not yet ascended to my Father; but go to my brethren and say to them, "I am ascending to my Father and your Father, and to my God and your God" (John 20:17).

Jesus appears the same evening to the disciples. They touch him and they eat together as he meets with them for forty days. He is in his glorified body, not bound by space, time, or locked doors; but He has yet to take his place at the right hand of God in the awesome glorified state in which he later appeared to Stephen (Acts 6-7), Paul (Acts 9:1-6), and John (Rev. 1:10-18). It would seem that He remained in some phase of the Ascension process and had not yet fully apprehended Exaltation.[5]

The Changing Position of Christ

Scripture makes it clear that Christ was present with God before Creation, that the world was made by or through him, and that it was made for his possession and his purpose. Within this context, however, a hierarchy clearly exists. The Son is always voluntarily in submission to God the Father, as is the Holy Spirit. Since the Holy Spirit is the instrument of Creation and the mode by which God's will is enacted, He must be subject both to the Father and the Son.[6] Therefore, that original hierarchy within the Godhead must have been Father / Son / Holy Spirit.

When Christ became incarnate, He did not lay down his divinity; but taking on the weakness of humanity, He apparently laid down for the time being his functional, authoritative position in the hierarchy. Jesus voluntarily subjected himself not only to the Father but to the Holy Spirit, being "made a little lower than the angels" (Heb. 2:7, 9) and emptying himself of all reputation (Phil. 2:6-8). While in the flesh, Jesus spoke only the words of the Father and did only the works of the Father, empowered by the Holy Spirit through voluntarily subjecting himself to him.[7] In a functional sense, the hierarchy had become Father / Holy Spirit / Son.

With the Ascension and Exaltation the original hierarchy was restored; but even more, Christ has done a marvelous work in exalting his Church within himself and under his authority. He now spiritually empowers his Church by the Holy Spirit in much the same way that He himself was empowered in his earthly ministry. One might conceive of a new, enhanced hierarchy, Father / Son / Holy Spirit / Church.

The Exaltation in John's Gospel

To John, Christ is the Word (*logos*, the wisdom, Reason, or order behind the universe) who was "with God" and "was divine" (John 1:1).[8] "All things were made through him, and nothing that was made was made without him" (1:3; see also Eph. 3:9-12, Col. 1:16-19).

Jesus declared to his disciples that "he who believes in me, the works that I do shall he do also; and greater works than these shall he do, because I go to my Father" (14:12). This idea is directly linked to it being "expedient that I go away; for if I do not go away, the [other] Comforter [like myself] will not come to you. But if I depart, I will send him to you" (16:7; insertions mine, see also 14:16).[9] For the Church to be empowered, Christ must go to the Father.

Why was it necessary for Christ to depart in order for the Holy Spirit to come in his fullness? Scripturally, it is God's plan to make Christ the Head of the Church and the giver of the Holy Spirit. In his incarnate body, however, He was the Christ in person but was finite, limited by the flesh. To perform his greater work, He must be exalted to the right hand of the Father's throne, where all God's power is committed unto him.[10] Christ is empowered by God in order to empower others through the Holy Spirit.

In John, the power is God's, the authority and message is Christ's, and the medium for the transmission of God's power is the Holy Spirit.

The Exaltation Present Throughout Scripture

The Exaltation of Christ is one of the most frequently recurring themes in Scripture. In Daniel, the Messiah is "a stone cut without hands" (2:34) who is "given dominion, glory, and a kingdom, that all people, nations, and tongues might serve him" (7:14). In Psalm 118:22, He is the stone that was "rejected" but "has become the head of the corner" (see also Isaiah 8:14-15, 28:16). Psalm 110:1, "The Lord (*YHWH*) said unto my Lord (*adonai*),[11] `Sit at my right hand, until I make your enemies your footstool'" is quoted in Matthew 22:44, Mark 12:36, Luke 20:42-43, Acts 2:34-35, and Hebrews

1:13. Christ is also declared to be positioned at the right hand of God in three Gospels, Acts, Romans, Ephesians, Colossians, Hebrews, and 1 Peter.[12]

In Romans, Christ was freed from the dominion of death, and now lives unto God (6:4-11), interceding for his own at God's right hand (8:34).   In First Corinthians, Christ is the foundation of his Church (3:11).   Christians are to be subject to Christ, as He is to God (3:23, 6:20, 8:6, 11:3). Spiritual gifts flow to the "Body" through the Holy Spirit, "dividing to each person individually" (12:11). God is the *source* of spiritual gifts (12:6, 18, 24, 28) but Christ is the *reason* (12:12, 27). Christ will one day subject all other powers and "all things" (*ta panta*)[13] to himself and turn them over to God (15:24-28).

In Ephesians, "all things" (*ta panta*) are consummated in Christ (1:10). God has seated him at his right hand above all rulers and authority (1:20-23). The Christ who *descended* also *ascended* in order to "fill" (*plerose*) "all things" (*ta panta*, 4:10). In Philippians, God has exalted Christ, giving him a name at which every knee must bow (2:9-11). One day, Christ will by his authority transform our mortal bodies (3:21).

In Colossians, all Creation is made by and for Christ. He is the "head" (*kephale*)[14] of the Church and embodies all "fullness" (*pleroma*) (1:16-19). Christ is the "head" of all rule and authority, and in him all the "fullness" of deity dwells (2:9-10).

While not intended to be exhaustive, this list demonstrates the pervasive and ubiquitous nature of the Exaltation theme.

In the Pattern of Ephesians 4:7-16

The process by which the exalted position of Christ is made manifest through spiritual gifts in the Church seems most explicit in this passage. Paul begins by using Psalm 68:18 to illustrate the process of Exaltation (4:8).[15] The same Jesus who *descended* to earthly existence is the same One who then *ascended* above the heavens. The reason He ascended is in order to "fill all things" and to dispense gifts to his Church (4:7, 8, 11).

These gifts are expressed here as persons who are spiritually gifted to fulfill the offices of the Church (4:11).[16] The purpose of the gifts are "the equipping of the saints" (4:12) and "that we might no longer be children" (4:14). The results of the gifts are to include service, edification, unity, knowledge of Christ, and maturity, achieving ultimately a "mature man" who somehow compares to the "fullness (*pleromatos*) of Christ" (4:13-15).[17] Throughout this process, each member is to be "supplied" by Christ through the working of the Spirit in and through the "Body," the Church (4:16).[18]

The "Fullness" of Christ

The study of the Exaltation of Christ will necessitate a thorough examination of Paul's use of the term "fullness" (*pleroma*). "Fullness" and such cognates as "fill," "full," "fulfill," etc., permeate Paul's writings. These are general terms entirely dependent upon their context, but in Paul they are sometimes theologically loaded. For example, the sense is possible that the "Body of Christ" (the Church) is *being filled* by the One who is himself already *full* (Ephesians 1:23, 3:19; *cf.* Col. 2:10).[19]

Spiritual Gifts (Charismata)

A theology emphasizing the Exaltation will necessitate an examination of spiritual gifts and gifting in that light. For instance, we must ask: is divine healing, which "is provided for in the Atonement,"[20] (1) automatic to every Christian (*i.e.*, "divine health"); (2) a charismatic gift, as Paul teaches; or (3) both?

I propose that the gifts *are provided* (*i.e.*, won, earned, established, etc.) through the Atonement, *administered by* Christ in his position of Exaltation, and *dispensed through* the Holy Spirit in the form of *charismata* (1 Cor. 12:9, 28, 30).

The Exaltation in the Head/Body Metaphors

Paul uses numerous metaphors to illustrate Christ's relationship to his Church, in which Christ is the figurative "Head" with the Church as his "Body." Paul, of course, often mixes his metaphors and terminology; but one might construct a synthesis of his head/body metaphors as follows:

Christ, as the "Head" ("ruler", *arche*) of all Creation, of all rule and authority, and of the Church, is also the authoritative and functional "head" (the body part, *kephale*): the leader, master, and controller of the "body." He is able, as the authority over the body, and as the Power of the universe, to provide for his Church in all things according to its needs (Eph. 1:22-23, 4:7-10; Col. 1:18, 2:10, 19).

As exalted Lord and ruler of the Church, Christ has joined it unto himself. He maintains perfect beneficence toward the Church, as a husband ("head" of the family) should his wife, wishing to nourish, cherish, and protect it (1 Cor.

11:3, Eph. 5:23). He accomplishes this by providing "gifts" to the Church, spiritually endowed but materially manifested among the individual believers.[21] These gifts are diversely distributed and serve to complement one another, as the various parts of a physical body cooperate to serve the whole (Rom. 12:3-18, 1 Cor. 12:12-30, Eph. 4:7-16, Col. 2:19). Thus, the "head" serves the "body," controlling it but also providing for it.

The supreme irony is that Christ is exalted Lord, yet He deigns with profound patience to serve the lowliest of those whom He rules.

Conclusion

A realization of the centrality and universality of Christ's Exaltation is essential to correct interpretation of Scripture. Much more study and application of this scriptural truth is needed on a broad base. But hopefully, this emphasis might in the future open many doors to the expansion, propagation, refinement, and in some cases correction, of Pentecostal doctrine.

NOTES

1. Paul A. Hughes, review of Delmer R. Guynes, *The Gospel of the Ascension* (Kuala Lumpur, Malaysia: Calvary Church Press, 1986), in *Paraclete* 26 (Fall 1992):30.

2. Heb. 2:8, *cf.* 1 Cor. 15:25.

3. See Dan. 7:13-14, Rev. 1:10-18, 14:14.

4. The popular doctrine that Jesus descended into hell while his body lay in the tomb, where He preached the Gospel to lost souls, "led captivity captive," and took from Satan the keys to hell and the grave, does not necessarily stand up to close exegetical scrutiny. In Ephesians 4:9, "the lower parts of the earth" to which Jesus descended before ascending (to heaven) need not refer to hell but to the tomb or, more likely, earthly existence. In 1 Peter 3:19-20, Christ via the Holy Spirit "preached to the spirits in prison" through Noah, the implication being not that Jesus preached during his 3 days in the tomb to those who had died in the Flood and were now in hell, but that He had already preached to them through Noah *before* the Flood. "The keys of Hades and of Death" (Rev. 1:18) taken into possession by the exalted Christ need not refer to literal keys but to his figurative and/or spiritual victory over death and the powers of hell through the Atonement; nor does the statement necessarily infer an incursion into Hades. Moreover, the presumption that Christ had to be condemned to hell in order to pay the debt for sin to God the Father encounters serious objections on many counts, and is not well founded in Scripture.

5. This question is further confused by Jesus' repeated assertions of being *already* glorified (John 13:3, 31; 16:15; *contra.* John 7:39, 12:16).

6. See for example Gen. 1:2, 6:3; Job 26:13; Mt. 1:18, 20; Lk. 12:12; John 16:13-15; Acts 1:2; Rom. 15:13.).

7. See Mt. 12:18; Luke 4:18; John 3:34-35, 7:16-19, 17:2; Acts 10:38 *et al.*

8. Some see in John 1 an echo of Genesis 1, in which God creates by the spoken word; though neither *logos* ("word," a noun) nor *lego* ("say," a verb) appears in Genesis 1 in the *Septuagint* (*LXX*), the Greek translation of the Hebrew Bible. Others see an intent to equate Christ with the Greek concept of divine Reason, similar to the attempt by the Alexandrian Jewish philosopher Philo to relate the *Logos* to the Hebrew God. Most likely, both ideas are present.

9. John 14:16 points out that the Comforter is *allon parakleton*, "another Paraclete." While *heteros* is "another of a different kind," *allos* is regularly "another of the same kind."

10. Just as Joseph was given all the power of Pharaoh, being subject only to Pharaoh himself (Genesis 41:39-44), Christ wields all the power of God, subject only to him.

11. The first "Lord" is *YHWH*, the "tetragrammaton" or "four-letter word" of God's name, generally pronounced "Yahweh." An earlier misunderstanding produced, via the German, the appellation "Jehovah." The second "Lord" is *adonai*, a term of deference applied to God, angels, or men, approximate to but slightly stronger than the English term "sir."

12. Mt. 26:64 (parallels Mk. 14:62, Lk. 22:69); Mk. 16:19; Acts 2:33, 7:55; Rom. 8:34; Eph. 1:20; Col. 3:1; Heb. 1:3, 8:1, 10:12, and 12:2; and 1 Peter 3:22.

13. Paul often places *ta panta*, "all things," equivalent to Creation (both material and spiritual) and in special relationship with "fullness" (*pleroma*) (see Eph. 1:9-10, 22-23, 4:10; Col. 1:16-20, 2:9-10; *cf.* 1 Cor. 10:26, 28).

14. Paul often uses *kephale*, "head," as equivalent to *arche*, "ruler," and *kurios*, "Lord" (see 1 Cor. 11:3, Eph. 1:17-23, 4:15, 5:22-24; Col. 1:15-19, 2:9-10, 19).

15. That Psalm 68:18 is used as illustration, not proof, is evident in his self-conscious alteration of "received gifts from men" to "gave gifts to men" (Eph. 4:8).

16. Compare Paul's mixing of charismatic gifts with gifted persons in 1 Cor. 12:7-11, 28-31. See also Rom. 12:3-8.

17. Eph. 4:13 could be rendered, "unto the measure of stature (full height) that pertains to Christ, which is characterized by fullness" (richness, completeness), wherein the mature ("perfect") man, or more likely the Church, is to somehow equal the "measure" ("standard") of Christ.

18. Compare the "vine" metaphor, John 15:1-8.

19. Interestingly, in Eph. 3:19, Christians are to be *filled* with the *fullness* of God; while in 4:12-13, they are to be *matured* to the *maturity* of Christ.

20. *Constitution of the Assemblies of God* (1993), article V, section 12. A 1974 position paper states that while healing is "in" and "flows from" the Atonement and is available to all believers, ultimate realization of immortality waits for our final redemption (Rom. 8:23) ("Divine Healing: An Integral Part of the Gospel" in *Where We Stand* [Springfield MO: Gospel Publishing House, 1990], 49-50). In other words, we are provided through Christ's Atonement with the *possibility* of divine healing, but not with a positive decree of *divine health* (immortality). See also Ansley Orfila, "A Thorn in the Flesh," *Paraclete* 18 (Summer 1984):29-32.

21. On the Baptism and spiritual gifts, see the author's "Speaking God's Message: the Holy Spirit and the Human Mind," *Paraclete* 26 (Spring 1992):17-22; and *Christ Within You! The Indwelling of the Holy Spirit* (Liberty, TX: Paul A. Hughes, 1993).

Chapter 24.   The Gnostic Christ

Gnosticism vs. Christianity

By the end of the second century, a religio-philosophical phenomenon on the fringes of Christianity had already been sharply defined by orthodox theologians and severely distanced from orthodox circles. This separation was performed expeditiously and effectively by such great orthodox leaders as Hippolytus, Tertullian, and most notably by Irenaeus in his *Against Heresies*.

This phenomenon is known today as Gnosticism. It was studied with interest in the twentieth century, especially since the discovery of a ruined Coptic library of Gnostic texts at Nag Hammadi in Egypt in 1947.

But why did the orthodox Church object so to this religious strain?   And why the renewed excitement among modern religion scholars?   The answer is the same on both counts: the thought of the Gnostics represents a variety of interpretation and application of the Christian message that differs from the orthodox view.

The most important point of departure from orthodox teaching is in the Gnostic redefinition of the meaning, purpose, and nature of Christ.

Is the Gnostic interpretation valid?   Is it indeed Christian?   Some liberal scholars consider it equally valid with the Christian message. The Gnostics, however, appear to be affected by considerable religious and philosophical thought that lies outside the Judeo-Christian orthodox continuum.   Perhaps the answer—or part of it—can be discovered by examining the sources of the Gnostic view of Christ, and the construct of Christ's nature and purpose they derive from those sources.

Definition of Terms

"Gnosticism" is a modern term[1] applied to a number of religious groups that placed an emphasis on esoteric knowledge (*gnōsis*) which is passed along, presumably, through the ages among those whom can be said to have "arrived," that is, achieved some higher spiritual plane.

One can refer to things "gnostic" in the broad sense or in the narrow sense.[2] The broad sense is most appropriately rendered "gnostic," with a lower-case "g", in that it refers to the fact of an esoteric knowledge, or to certain traits or tendencies generally associated with known Gnostic religions. In this way, New Testament passages might be, and often are, alleged to be "gnosticizing." Two examples are: (1) references to the Gospel as "saving knowledge"; and (2) the use of terminology—notably by Paul—such as "knowledge," "all things" (*tá pánta*, e.g., "the All"), "fullness" (*plērōma*), etc., which were at times employed as Gnostic technical terms.

Conversely, it is appropriate to refer to traits, practices, elements, etc., as "Gnostic," with a capital "G", when applied to what is by definition a specifically Gnostic religion. A working definition of Gnostic religion will follow in the next section.

Two more terms must be contrasted: "pre-Gnostic" and "proto-Gnostic." According to the definition adopted at the Messina congress on Gnostic origins in 1966, "pre-Gnostic" refers to elements that existed before Christianity and were later incorporated into Gnostic religions. A "proto-Gnostic" element, on the other hand, is one that belongs specifically to the early stages of the formation of a Gnostic religion.[3]

Finally, one last term may now be defined, that is, "pre-Christian Gnosticism." In the twentieth century, there was considerable debate whether (1) Gnosticism as a religion preceded and developed in parallel or even in tandem with Christianity; or (2) it developed more or less directly from Christianity and existed as a Christian heresy.

The view of Gnosticism as a Christian heresy prevailed until at least 1909, when Robert Law proposed Hellenistic-Oriental Gnostic origins.[4] Later, Rudolf Bultmann became a major figure in a school of thought (following Richard Reitzenstein's hypothesis) that saw Gnosticism as both preceding and affecting Christianity,[5] and Gnosticism as equally valid from *religionsgeschicte* point-of-view. To call Gnosticism "pre-Christian" implies a view similar to Bultmann's.

In recent years, the pendulum has largely swung back to a more medial position. Bultmann's proposed Iranian origin of Gnosticism is today almost universally rejected.[6] Many scholars recognize pre-Christian elements having been incorporated into Gnosticism, but are critical of theories of a pre-Christian Gnostic religion such as that Bultmann constructed from post-Christian sources.

Delineation of Gnostic Religion

Because of the extensive variety of Gnostic and gnosticizing groups, it is necessary to provide a basic definition of Gnostic religion. In a 1967 article, T. P. van Baaren suggested in sixteen points the characteristics of Gnostic religion.[7] His points, however, are complex and sometimes overlap, and in some cases apply specific characteristics too broadly.[8] About the same time, H. Goedicke listed just four points,[9] which yet do not seem sufficiently in-depth. A more practical delineation of Gnostic religion is as follows:

1. A transcendent and impersonal God rules the heavens.

2. The material world is evil (*i.e.*, *cosmological dualism*).

3. Man has fallen from a pure pneumatic (*i.e.*, spiritual) state into the evil material realm.

4. God and the material realm are separated by a spiritual realm (the *plērōma*), filled with intermediate beings (*aeons*, "emanations," or "hypostases").

5. The material world is ruled by an evil *archōn* or *archōns* ("rulers") or Demiurge.

6. God at times sends redeemers to man to reveal a saving *gnōsis*.

7. Through the esoteric *gnōsis*, man is able to save himself, regain his spiritual (pneumatic) nature, and in the end ascend to his place in the *plērōma*.

8. This salvation is available to a limited number of "elect" pneumatics.

This formulation should now provide a workable definition from which to continue this study.

Origins of the Gnostic Redeemer Figure

Most Gnostic redemption myths begin with the fall of Sophia ("Wisdom") to the earthly realm. This personified Wisdom figure might have been drawn directly from Old Testament and Apocryphal sources,[10] or from even more ancient Hebrew-Canaanite traditions.[11]

Sophia persuades the Demiurge, the evil creator of the material world, to give life to Adam,[12]—to the Naassene and Barbelo sects the "Primal Man."[13] This Primal Man is identified by Bultmann as originating with the Iranian Primal Man/Redeemer myth.[14] Bultmann has considered Mandaean texts to contain skeletal remnants of a more ancient Iranian prototype.[15] However, he commits a fundamental error in constructing a pre-Christian myth from post-Christian sources alone[16]—no extant Gnostic text can reasonably be dated earlier than the second century.[17]

Similarly, E. F. Scott postulates the origin of the Gnostic Primal Man in "some primitive myth, the meaning of which can now only be conjectured, and which possibly underlies the imagery of Daniel and the Book of Enoch."[18] Here two hypotheses are yet to be established: (1) that Daniel and Enoch indeed utilized a more ancient myth; and (2) that the later Gnostic myth in turn descended from that of Daniel and Enoch.

Depending upon the specific variety of Gnosticism, either Sophia or the Primal Man exist in a fallen state[19] and require redemption. Until their redemption, the spiritual and material worlds co-exist in tension, in an imperfect and unacceptable state of admixture. At the prayer of Sophia (or "on his own initiative" in the Naassene material)[20] a Redeemer ("an Aeon of supreme rank—the Soter or Christus")[21] descends into the material world to rescue the fallen one. There are in fact numerous redeemer figures identified in gnostic and related literature.[22] From Judaism, directly or indirectly, come the figures of "the Great Seth" or "Illuminator";[23] Melchizedek/Seth;[24] the *descensus angelorum* (allegorized by Philo);[25] the "Light" or "Man" of Ezekiel;[26] the "Son of Man" of Daniel;[27] and certainly the figures of Jewish messianism and apocalyptic.[28] The "Teacher of Righteousness" of the Qumran sect (ostensibly Essene) has also been cited—but the Qumranians were essentially apocalyptists rather than Gnostics.

From Mesopotamia come many redeemer figures, notably Marduk and Mithra; and from Egypt, Osiris.[29]

Various Hellenistic sources are postulated. In Plato is found the Ideal Man, though the redemptive idea is absent.[30] It is alleged that in some Middle Platonic sources that "the translator of Ezekiel [1:26] in the Septuagint identifies the figure of divine Man with the Platonic idea."[31] The Hermetic *Poimandres* (Hellenistic Jewish) posits an androgynous Phos/Zoe figure who descends and spawns mankind; Philo identifies the Divine Man or "Man of

God" with the Logos.[32] However, only certain Gnostic systems coupled the Logos figure with the redeemer function. In other systems, Logos remained an entirely separate entity.[33]

The foregoing redeemer figures, with the exception of Philo and the Hermetic writings, do indeed represent pre-Christian elements alleged to later affect Gnosticism; yet none truly exhibits evidence of a Gnostic religion preceding Christianity, *i.e.*, "pre-Christian Gnosticism."

Redeemers more specific to Gnosticism are identified in Gnostic writings. "In the system of Simon Magus, Simon himself is the redeemer and appears in one form as Jesus."[34] *Pistis Sophia*, 369, refers to "Zorokothora-Meljisedek," according to F. C. Burkitt a corrupted coupling of the names Zoroaster and Melchizedek—but not in fact having anything to do with the historical characters. Only their names have been borrowed.[35]

John Dart describes two Gnostic redeemers which he considers to be in no way patterned after Jesus Christ. Derdekeas, in *The Paraphrase of Shem*, is touted as a "divine warrior" after the model of the Canaanite *Ba'al* or the Hebrew *Yahweh*.[36] In Dart's description, he seems to be nothing more than a fallen *aeon*, but does at times take on some function as Redeemer (or "Revealer").[37] The *Apocalypse of Adam* presents one called the Illuminator as a redeemer.[38] This figure does indeed (against Dart) appear to be based on a re-staging of the Incarnation and Passion of Jesus. The Gnostic writings appear to adapt redeemer figures after either of two patterns: (1) ancient historical/mythological/philosophical/legendary figures; or (2) the Christian presentation of Jesus Christ.

The Nature of Gnostic Redemption

Redemption in Gnosticism is not legal, ethical, or apocalyptic, as it appears variously in Judaism and Christianity. Gnosticism appears to be based on Persian physical dualism (*i.e.*, light versus darkness), but modified into a cosmological dualism of spiritual versus material.[39] The Gnostics hoped to transfer from this world to the spiritual realm, and ultimately into the *plērōma*, by the receipt of an esoteric *gnōsis*, *i.e.*, "spiritual enlightenment."[40] This *gnōsis* was brought, directly or indirectly, by a redeemer who acted as "revealer" to a select few of the "elect."

To the Gnostics, being awakened from their sleep and perceiving the knowledge, "gnosis," of their beginnings and destiny was "redeeming" for them. In other words, obtaining mystical knowledge of this kind was thought to be their salvation, and in that sense a revealer-figure was also a redeemer.[41]

The Gnostic Christ

Not all Gnostics cared to associate themselves with the figure of Jesus Christ. The Mandaeans are a sect that venerated John the Baptist, but rejected Jesus as a false prophet.[42]

Still, overall the Gnostics freely and readily adopted the Christ-image as their Redeemer, or the latest in a series of redeemers. "The grand characteristic of Christian Gnosticism is the identification of the mythical Redeemer with Christ, with whose history the pagan traditions are interwoven."[43]   Jesus became to them a mystical figure: one who, according to the Valentinians, clothed himself with the esoteric "Name of the Lord."[44]

Jesus did not, say the Gnostics, come to bear the sins of men, that whoever believes in his atoning death may gain eternal life. "The real purpose of Jesus, or rather of the *Soter* ['Savior'] who used Him as his instrument, was to communicate the hidden *gnōsis*."[45]

Most scholars consider the general Gnostic view of the Incarnation to be *docetic* (from Gk. *dokein*, "to seem"). This term, however, is usually applied to the early heretical position that Jesus was never actually present in the flesh, but only "seemed" to be human. He was, in this view, entirely spiritual and his human appearance an illusion. Thus Elaine Pagels is probably right in objecting to the docetic label.[46]

Instead, the Gnostic Christ had two natures: the *pneumatic* (spiritual) and the *psychic* (physiological).   The Gnostics variously held that the Savior/Redeemer indwelt the earthly Jesus at birth (the Naassenes and the *Pistis Sophia*), at the age of twelve (the Justinians), or at his baptism by John (most sects).[47]   The Valentinians believed that at his baptism Jesus received the "Name of the Lord."[48]   The divine Savior departed from Jesus' body at the time of the trial before Pilate,[49] later while on the cross, or somewhere in-between. Basilides taught that Simon of Cyrene was transformed to look like Jesus and crucified in his place.[50] Such separation of Christ from the material world was evidently requisite in order to comply with Gnostic dualistic conceptions.

Thus the true (Gnostic) Christ escaped suffering and death.[51]   Christ's death was not a redemptive act: it was merely due to an outburst of wrath from the evil Demiurge.[52]   The wholly spiritual Christ—according to Basilides, *The Second Treatise of the Great Seth*, and *The Apocalypse of Peter*—now laughed at the folly of his would-be executors.[53] They thought they could rid themselves of the divine Redeemer!

> He whom you see above the tree, glad and laughing, is the
> living Jesus. But the one into whose hands and feet they
> drive the nails is his fleshly part, which is the substitute . . .
> one made in his likeness.[54]

This "laughing" of Christ was possibly drawn from Psalm 2, concerning those who conspired "against the Lord and his Anointed," so that "He who sits in the heavens laughs; the Lord has them in derision."[55]

Summary

The Redeemer figure is one variously assembled from ancient myths and traditions. Then the figure of Jesus Christ was adapted and fitted into the Gnostic scheme as yet another redeemer. Just as Gnostic teachers appropriated Paul's terminology to their purposes, they also appropriated the figure of Christ.

The evidence adduced here does not suggest a Gnostic religion preceding Christianity—not as defined. There might have existed gnosticizing traits in some pre-Christian religious sects. There might be elements and terminology in primitive Christianity itself that can be called Gnostic. Yet, Gnosticism as we know it from Nag Hammadi and related texts cannot be demonstrated before Christianity was well established.

Gnosticism is by nature syncretistic.[56] The Gnostic Jesus presented here is the natural byproduct of this syncretism, wherein elements pre-Christian and post-Christian; elements Egyptian, Iranian, Hellenistic, philosophical, etc.; and elements derived from specious exegesis and active imaginations have melded to produce a radically different Christ from that of orthodox Christianity—and one that is just as naturally labeled heretical by its opponents.

Notes

1. See Casey (JTS XXXVI [1938], 60), cited by R. McLaglan Wilson, "Gnostic Origins," *Vigiliae Christianae* 9 (1955):195, see also 193.

2. See Edwin M. Yamauchi, *Pre-Christian Gnosticism*, 2d ed. (Grand Rapids: Baker Book House, 1983), 16 f.

3. Ibid., 18.

4. Wilson, "Gnostic Origins," 194.

5. See Edwin M. Yamauchi, "Jewish Gnosticism?" in *Studies in Gnosticism and Hellenistic Religions*, ed. R. van den Broek and M. J. Vermaseren (Leiden: E. J. Brill, 1981), 469-477.

6. See Wilson, "Gnostic Origins, " 194, 207; Gilles Quispel, "Gnosticism from Its Origins to the Middle Ages," in *The Encyclopedia of Religion*, vol. 5, ed. Mircea Eliade (NY: Macmillan Publishing Co., 1987), 568; and G. Quispel, "Gnosticism and the New Testament,," *Vigiliae Christianae* 19 (1965):73.

7. T. P. van Baaren, "Toward a Definition of Gnosticism," in U. Bianchi, ed., Le *Origini dello Gnosticismo* (1967), 178-180, quoted in Yamauchi, *Pre-Christian*, 14 f.

8. Yamauchi, *Pre-Christian*, 14 f.

9. Ibid.,15.

10. See Yamauchi, "Jewish Gnosticism?" 489-90.

11. See Quispel, "From Its Origins," 568.

12. Ibid., 570.

13. E. F. Scott, "Gnosticism," in *Encyclopaedia of Religion and Ethics*, vol. 6, ed. James Hastings (NY: Charles Scribner's Sons, 1955), 236.

14. Henry A. Green, "Gnosis and Gnosticism: A Study in Methodology," *Numen* 24 (August 1977):117.

15. Ibid., 116.

16. Ibid., 116 f., 123.

17. See C. H. Dodd, *The Interpretation of the Fourth Gospel*, 98, paraphrased in Wilson, "Gnostic Origins," 205; Dodd is followed here against Wilson's own (unjustified) dating of Christian Gnostic origins to the mid-first century.

18. Scott, 236.

19. *The Apocryphon of John* even "combines the Anthropos ["Man"] model and the Sophia model," Quispel, "From Its Origins," 570.

20. Scott, 237.

21. Ibid.

22. See Yamauchi, *Pre-Christian*, 168.

23. Gedaliahu A. G. Stroumsa, *Another Seed: Studies in Gnostic Mythology*, Nag Hammadi Studies, vol. 24, ed. Martin Krause, James M. Robinson, and Frederik Wisse (Leiden: E. J. Brill, 1984), 110.

24. Ibid., 111; see also Yamauchi, "Jewish Gnosticism?" 488.

25. Wilson, "Gnostic Origins," 203.

26. Quispel, "From Its Origins," 567.

27. Ibid.

28. G. van Groningen, *First Century Gnosticism: Its Origin and Motifs* (Leiden: E. J. Brill, 1967), 70-72.

29. Scott, 237.

30. *Cf.* Quispel, "From Its Origins," 567 f.; see also Yamauchi, "Jewish Gnosticism?" 494; and Wilson, *The Gnostic Problem* (London: A. R. Mowbray and Co., 1958), 221, 226.

31. Quispel, "From Its Origins," 568.

32. Ibid.

33. Yamauchi, "Jewish Gnosticism?" 480.

34. Wilson, *Gnostic Problem*, 226.

35. F. C. Burkitt, *Church and Gnosis* (Cambridge, Eng.: Cambridge University Press, 1932), 69.

36. John Dart, *The Laughing Savior* (NY: Harper and Row, 1976), 97-101.

37. Ibid., 100 f.

38. Ibid., 101-103.

39. Scott, 234.

40. Ibid.

41. Dart, 101.

42. Yamauchi, "Jewish Gnosticism?" 469, 471.

43. Scott, 237.

44. Quispel, "New Testament," 80, see also 82.

45. Scott, 237.

46. Elaine H. Pagels, "Gnostic and Orthodox views of Christ's Passion: Para-digms for the Christian's Response to Persecution?" in *The Rediscovery of Gnosticism*, vol. 1, ed. Bentley Layton, *Studies in the History of Religions*, vol. 41, ed. M. H. van Voss, E. J. Sharpe, and R. J. Z. Werblowsky (Leiden: E. J. Brill, 1980), 264.

47. Scott, 237

48. Quispel, "New Testament," 80.

49. Pagels, 265.

50. Dart, 108-109.

51. See Irenaeus, *Against Heresies* 3.16.6; according to Pagels, however, the Valentinians affirmed the Passion of Christ, Pagels, 262-88; but the spiritual part of Christ still did not suffer only the psychic (266).

52. Scott, 237.

53. Dart, 109.

54. From *The Apocalypse of Peter*, quoted in Dart, 107.

55. Ibid.

56. See Dodd, *Fourth Gospel*, 97 f., quoted in Wilson, "Gnostic Origins," 197.

Chapter 25. Worship in the Second Century

The Spiritual Dimension[*]

Much study has been devoted to the forms of worship in the primitive Church. Scholars have painstakingly detailed the practices of baptism and the Eucharist. They have studied the evolution of worship services from the Sabbath to Sunday, examined the controversies surrounding the Easter observance, and developed great taxonomies of orthodox worship.

In the midst of all this, there are more practical concerns in the minds of everyday Christians. Some seek continuity with the early disciples of Christ in the worship experience through religious form. Because this emphasis is ultimately empty and powerless, however, many are forsaking vacuous religiosity for a truer relationship with God in Christ, a worship "in spirit and in truth." They are searching, not for correct form, but for correct response toward God.

This article is intended to examine the worship of (roughly) the second century. It will attempt to demonstrate a continuity of this spiritual worship with that of the Apostles and the New Testament Church, and to describe the workings of this worship, which was indeed spiritual rather than mechanical, and personal as well as corporate.

Prayer

Prayer is generally considered the most basic component of worship and spiritual living. In the second century, prayer was practiced in numerous capacities. Perhaps the most common of these mentioned in early Christian writings was the ceremonial prayer. These prayers, formulated for such formal or corporate occasions as baptism, the Eucharist, and the Lord's Day gathering,[1] were not intended to instill dry formalism into the Church, although they seem to have contributed to its germination. Instead, they served first to acknowledge the sovereignty of God and the Sonship of Jesus Christ.[2] Thankfulness for both the gift of salvation and daily provision was also a prominent feature of ceremonial prayers.[3] These acknowledgments were

[*]Originally published in *Paraclete* 21 (Fall 1987):20-25.

intended to honor God not by ritual but by directing the worshipers' hearts and minds toward the Divine. This in turn would edify the participants by stirring up faith and causing them to dwell upon the pure things of God.[4]

Individual prayer also seems to have been universally prescribed. Christians were encouraged to pray at least three times a day.[5] Prayers were to be individual and heartfelt, rather than ritualistic.[6] Tertullian insisted that, even in group prayer, Christians do not need a leader since their prayers come from their hearts.[7]

The content of prayer included a request for guidance,[8] daily provision,[9] and special comfort and strength.[10] Yet, the most frequent subject of prayer mentioned in second-century writings is intercession for others. Clement encouraged the Corinthians to pray for both the physical and spiritual well-being of others.[11] The *Didache* instructed Christians to pray for their persecutors[12] and further said, "Do not hate anybody; but reprove some, pray for others, and still others love more than your own life."[13] Justin claimed that Christians always prayed for their enemies.[14] The Apologists often mentioned that the Church prayed for Caesar and the welfare of his empire.[15]

The most common posture for both prayer and praise seems to have been with arms outstretched, "lifting holy hands."[16] This was done variously while standing[17] or kneeling.[18] The custom of lifting the hands may have been adopted from Judaism, or more directly from the New Testament references.[19] Perhaps this point in itself fittingly demonstrates the continuity of practice from Apostolic times into the second century. Nevertheless, none of this seems to be arbitrary, a matter of form devoid of rationale. Tertullian aptly wrote, "Looking up to Him, we Christians—with hands extended, because they are harmless, with head bare because we are not ashamed . . . ."[20]

Prayer, especially intercession, was often accompanied by fasting. Because fasting is a relatively minor issue in the New Testament, the primitive Church might have taken precedent from Old Testament Judaism. While fasting was also an element of pagan worship, Tertullian was quick to separate its function and purpose in Christianity from the pagan practice. He stated, "Superstition demands that a fast be imposed on those consulting an incubation-oracle, so as to achieve the proper degree of ritual purity." He added:

> Daniel ate dry food for a period of three weeks, but he did
> this in order to win God's favor by acts of humiliation and
> not that he might augment the perception and mental vision

of his soul as a preparation for a dream, as though the soul were meant to act without being in a state of ecstacy. Sobriety, then, will have no effect of neutralizing the ecstacy, but of recommending the ecstacy to God so that it might take place in Him.[21]

Fasting can thus be seen as a way to move the heart of God through self-abasement—always accompanied by earnest prayer. A similar idea was Clement's: "Let us prostrate ourselves before him as suppliants of his mercy and kindness."[22] Fasting also seems to have been a general requirement just prior to baptism, an integral part of the ceremony of purification and re-birth.[23]

Several final comments are in order in regard to fasting. Many today would object to the necessity of fasting, considering it to be attributable to pagan influence, or else an element of obsolete Judaic legalism. Certainly, its favor seems to have varied from place to place in the second century. The early Montanists, for example, were especially ascetic—much more so than was the rule—as were many Jewish Christians.[24] Likewise, Philo related the extreme ascetic practices of a group he called Therapeutae, who abounded around Alexandria, whom Eusebius further identified as early Christians.[25]

Outside of these extremists, however, there is no reason to assume that fasting was a major issue. In fact, such things often suffered ill repute.[26] If there was then any orthodox view, it would seem to be that fasting was used merely as a tool for setting aside the things of the flesh for a little while, concomitant with a special need or occasion, to give attention to the things of God. This is indeed a worthy endeavor and seems to represent the ultimate concern of the early writers as a whole.

Praise and Worship

Among the second-century writers, praise, worship, and adoration are largely viewed together with prayer rather than separately. Justin, for instance, spoke of "praising him by the word of prayer and thanksgiving for all that he has given us."[27] Raising the hands, kneeling, crying out, fasting, acknowledging God in word or deed are all acts of worship, although integral with the practice of prayer.

Yet, a few specific ideas can profitably be highlighted: Thanksgiving is an important part of praise, acknowledging God and Christ for the things they have done. Prominent among the writings was giving thanks to God for the great gift of his Son.[28] The writers went further to thank Him for all manner of provision, ". . . for our creation and all the means of health, for the variety of creatures and the changes of seasons . . . ."[29] The entire Christian life is to be one of gratefulness toward God.

Another aspect of Christian worship was the practice of morality and kindness, both among the Christians themselves and toward others. As the Apostle Paul exhorted New Testament Christians to be blameless in the midst of a perverse world, so also did the Christian leaders of the second century.[30] Ignatius insisted that the Magnesians should not identify with Christ in name only, but must *be* Christians.[31] Justin commended the practice of sharing with one another and charity toward the less fortunate, as also did Polycarp.[32] The *Didache* declared, "Let your donation sweat in your hands until you know to whom to give it."[33] Through kindness, mercy, and godliness, the Christian was to honor God, demonstrate the love of God to the outside world, and fulfill the divine law of love.

Songs of praise were used as an aid to worship, just as they had been in the New Testament.[34] The Roman governor Pliny the Younger related to Caesar that the Christians "met regularly before dawn on a fixed day to chant verses alternately among themselves in honor of Christ. . . ."[35] Justin described the Church "in thankfulness to him sending up solemn prayers and hymns . . . ."[36] Such songs no doubt were designed to focus attention upon the person and deeds of God and Jesus Christ (as were the many other acts of worship). Moreover, they served by their very nature to unify the thoughts and attitudes, as well as actions, of the participants as they gathered together for fellowship, corporate worship, and intercessory prayer.

Charismata

The most controversial element of second-century worship is in regard to the perpetuation of the charismatic gifts from Apostolic times. Without launching into polemics, it appears self-evident that prophetic gifts and related phenomena were active in this period. In keeping with the purposes of this article, however, our discussion will be limited to their contribution to worship.

The *charismata* which Paul enumerated in 1 Corinthians 12-14 are many and varied. All of them in a sense can be considered acts of worship. Yet the gifts which seem to lend themselves most readily to worship are tongues and prophecy.

Tongues, according to Paul, were an individual expression of worship toward God.[37] But these tongues, inspired by the Holy Spirit, could likewise be made intelligible by inspired interpretation, serving to edify the hearers.[38] What Paul termed prophecy seems to be approximate in content and purpose to an interpreted utterance in tongues.[39] These manifestations were divine utterances serving to build up the congregation by exhorting, comforting, and otherwise edifying them.[40]

In the second-century writings, these gifts were frequently mentioned as being currently manifested among the Christians. The *Didache* spoke of prophets making ecstatic utterances.[41] Ignatius claimed to be speaking inspired messages on various occasions.[42] Athenagoras referred to prophets being active in the Church in his day.[43] Irenaeus, writing late in the second century, further mentioned that there were those in the Church who were presently speaking in diverse languages through the Holy Spirit.[44]

If there was a decline in the practice of these manifestations during this period, it seems to be due to efforts by the bishops to consolidate their authority by limiting the official, authoritative, "inspired" utterance to themselves and to their office.[45] But in direct opposition to this trend are numerous testimonies of charismatic gifts being exercised continually and universally in orthodox Christianity.[46] What, after all, could be more comforting, more faith-inspiring, more worshipful and praise-evoking than a word of comfort or exhortation which by the very nature of its delivery is testified to be divine? Just as the Lord revitalized his apostles by pouring out the Holy Spirit upon them, the Church could enjoy continual renewal and sustaining grace as they encountered and utilized his Spirit in their worship.

Conclusion

Second-century worship, like that of the New Testament, was primarily spiritual, concerned with the proper relationship toward God. The Church had not yet developed a highly formalized worship, although incipient formalism was visible. Instead, the individual Christian was concerned with living a holy, charitable, and worship-filled life, honoring God in all he did and all he was. He regularly gave homage to his Lord, and in doing so fully expected to receive from Him comfort, encouragement, and exhortation by the Holy Spirit of promise.

Worship was not arbitrary: the acts performed in worship had a rationale behind them. For instance, the posture used in prayer had an underlying meaning, and fasting a higher purpose than simply complying to form. The ultimate criteria were true worship and service to God and their Savior.

Indeed, "we who are alive and remain" would do well to remember these factors when tempted to adhere to forms and traditions that are in fact meaningless apart from true worship of the heart. Our link with the first Christians is not in doing what they did and saying what they said, but in having our own relationship with Christ, and truly worshipping Him "in spirit and in truth."

Notes

1. See, for example, *Didache* 9.1-10.6.

2. See *Didache* 9.3-4 and Justin *Apology* I 13, 65, 67; *cf.* Irenaeus *Against Heresies* 5.2.1-3.

3. See *Didache* 8.2, and Tertullian *Prayer*.

4. *Cf.* Philippians 4:6-9. This was also the purpose of singing psalms and hymns, as in Ephesians 5:18-20.

5. See *Didache* 8.3; and Tertullian *De Oratione* 25.5-26. Hippolytus commends seven prayer times daily (*Apostolic Tradition* 4.35, 36).

6. See Athenagoras *Plea* 13.

7. Tertullian *Apology* 30.4.

8. See 1 Clement 61:1-3.

9. See *Didache* 8.2.

10. See Ignatius *Trallians* 12.3, 13.3.

11. 1 Clement 2:6, 56:1, 59:4.

12. *Didache* 1.3.

13. *Didache* 2.7.

14. Justin *Apol.* I 67; *cf.* Tert. *Apol.* 31.2.

15. See Athen. *Plea* 37; and Tert. *Apol.* 30.4, 31.1-33.2.

16. See 1 Clement 2:3; and Athen. *Plea* 13.

17. See Just. *Apol.* I 67.

18. See Tert. *Apol.* 30.7.

19. See 1 Timothy 2:8.

20. Tert. *Apol.* 30.4.

21. Tert. *On the Soul* 48.3, 4.

22. 1 Clement 9:1; *cf.* Tert. *Apol.* 40.15.

23. See *Didache* 7; and Just. *Apol.* I 61.

24. On Montanism, see Roy J. Deferrari et al., eds., *Eusebius Pamphili: Ecclesiastical History*, trans. Roy J. Deferrari (Washington, D.C.: The Catholic University of America Press, 1953), p. 322n; and on Jewish Christianity, see George W. Buchanan, "Worship, Feasts, and Ceremonies in the Early Jewish-Christian Church," *New Testament Studies* 26 (April 1980):279-80; *cf.* Ignatius *Magnesians* 8.1, 9.1.

25. Eusebius *Ecclesiastical History* 2.17.

26. Euseb. *Eccl. Hist.* 5.18; and *Letter to Diognetus* 4.1.

27. Just. *Apol.* I 13.

28. *Didache* 9.3; Ignatius *Smyrneans* 1.1; Iren. *AH* 10.1; and *Martyrdom of Polycarp* 14.

29. Just. *Apol.* I 13; *cf.* 1 Clem. 19, 20.

30. See *Letter of Polycarp* 2.1-11.4; and 1 Clem. 48:1-50:7.

31. Ignatius *Magnesians* 4.

32. Just. *Apol.* I 67, and *Letter of Polycarp* 10.

33. A saying of unknown origin, quoted in *Didache* 1.6.

34. See Acts 16:25, Ephesians 5:19, and Colossians 3:16.

35. Pliny *Epistles* 10.96.7, Loeb Classical Library, p. 289.

36. Just. *Apol.* I 13, *EC Fathers*, p. 249; see also Euseb. *Eccl. Hist.* 2:17, *The Fathers of the Church* 19, pp. 113, 114, 116.

37. See 1 Corinthians 14:2, 14, 17.

38. See 1 Cor. 14:14-16. Such expressions were, however, sometimes in a human language which could be understood by those familiar with it, see Acts 2:4-11.

39. See 1 Cor. 14:5, 13.

40. See 1 Cor. 14:3, 12, 19, 26, 31.

41. *Didache* 11.7.

42. Ignatius *Trall.* 4.1, *Romans* 8.3, *Philadelphians* 7.1, 2.

43. Athen. *Plea* 7, 10.

44. Iren. *AH* 5.6.1.

45. For a discussion of this viewpoint, see James L. Ash, Jr., "The Decline of Ecstatic Prophecy in the Early Church," *Theological Studies* 36 (June 1976):227-52; see also Erich Nestler, "Was Montanism a Heresy?" *Pneuma* 6 (Spring 1984):67-78.

46. See Ignatius *To Polycarp* 2.2; Just. *Apol.* I 36; Iren. *AH* 3.11.9, 5.20.1, 2; Iren. *Proof of the Apostolic Preaching* 99; Epiphanius *Panarion* 48.1; Euseb. *Eccl. Hist.* 5.17; and Origen *Against Celsus* 1.46.

Chapter 26.   Are the Anti-Pentecostal Arguments Valid?

The Case of 1 Corinthians 12-14[*]

. . . we believe that students who are a part of the modern-day tongues movement should seek their college education elsewhere as they would not be allowed to participate in or promote any charismatic activities.

—1994-95 catalog, Pensacola Christian College, p. 8.

Note: For purposes of this article, the term "Pentecostal" is used to refer to anyone who accepts and practices Pentecostal/charismatic gifts. The term "anti-Pentecostal" refers to those who argue against the validity of such gifts, "speaking in tongues" in particular.

G. Campbell Morgan called it "the last vomit of Satan." To Dr. Reuben Torrey, it was "emphatically not of God."[1] Historically, many of those who practice this phenomenon have been ostracized from their churches and denominations. What could possibly elicit such a vehement response? Pentecostalism, of course.

Non-Pentecostals have traditionally denounced the so-called Tongues Movement and all related practices. They base their opposition on certain passages from the Bible—the same passages, in many cases, that Pentecostals use as part or their own theological foundations. It has often been assumed that, since the mainline denominations can summon the authority of numerous scholars in big-name schools, this "weight of scholarship" certainly proves that the orthodox interpretations are correct. But is this necessarily so? When a seminary student begins to study Greek exegesis, he is informed that the majority of manuscript "witnesses" to a particular reading do not always attest the most reliable reading. Likewise, the majority

---

[*] Originally submitted to Dr. Gary B. McGee, The Assemblies of God Theological Seminary, May 28, 1985.

opinions does not necessarily prove an argument.   The majority can be mistaken.

Anti-Pentecostals make many claims from Scripture, as well as from other sources. These claims have been widely publicized, and generally accepted by many Christians. But are they valid? In this study, each of the major anti-Pentecostal arguments in regard to 1 Corinthians 12-14 will be evaluated on its own merit to determine its strengths and weaknesses. Then perhaps the reader will be better equipped to decide the issue for himself.

The Biblical Foundations of Tongues-Speaking

Throughout the Bible, the Holy Spirit gave special power to God's servants. He gave special wisdom to kings, and superhuman strength to some like Samson. He enabled the prophets to speak out God's words with authority, as well as to predict future events. But this divine power and authority was not given to all who believed, only to those whom God chose. He anointed prophets, priests, and kings with the power of his Spirit.

However, God promised Israel that the day would come when He would "pour out [His] spirit upon all flesh" (Joel 2:28; cf. Isaiah 30:21; Jeremiah 31:33; Ezekiel 11:19-20, 37:14). The Holy Spirit would dwell in the hearts of all the faithful and teach them directly, just as the prophets were taught (John 14:26, 16:13-15).

Many commentators ascribe this prediction to the coming Kingdom Age. In that case, was Peter misapplying Scripture at Pentecost when he identified the strange occurrence of "other tongues" as "that which was said by the prophet Joel" (Acts 2:16)? Certainly, there are serious problems in trying to say that Pentecost was the total fulfillment of the prophecy (though both sides of the controversy have done so). After all, where were the "signs and wonders" Joel predicted, like the darkening of the sun, and the moon turned blood-red? John MacArthur, Jr., suggests that the Spirit's outpouring in Acts was a "preview" or "pre-fulfillment" of what is yet to take place in the future Kingdom Age.[2] This perspective, however, intimates that other New Testament "tongues," including those in Corinth, were not genuine; and such a "pre-fulfillment" is never so much as hinted at in Scripture. Moreover, in proposing a "pre-fulfillment" of a later "dispensation," i.e., that of the Kingdom, MacArthur seems to violate his own dispensational stance.

In his book, *Exegetical Fallacies*, D. A. Carson suggests that Peter did not mean that the occurrence at Pentecost was the literal fulfillment of Joel 2:28ff.[3] Perhaps Peter was merely identifying Pentecost as the same *type* of outpouring. In any case, Peter does not seem to be at all surprised that Joel's "signs and wonders," other than tongues of fire over their heads and speaking in unknown languages, did not occur.

When the Spirit came upon the disciples, they spoke with "other tongues." Jews and proselytes from faraway lands, gathered to Jerusalem for the great Feast of Firstfruits (Pentecost), were amazed when each one heard praises to God in his own native language, spoken fluently by these unlearned Galileans. Others (*heteroi*, "others of a different kind," *i.e.*, not the same Jews) mocked them, saying they were drunk. Nevertheless, through both this sign and Peter's preaching, three thousand people were convinced and added to the church.

Elsewhere in Acts, the occurrence of tongues is repeated (10:44-46, 19:6), and at least implied in 4:31, 8:12-17, and 11:15. In other instances, it is unclear whether "baptism" refers to Holy Spirit baptism or water baptism (9:18, 16:15, 18:18, etc.). Other Spirit-endowed gifts are evident in the Acts, such as healings and the casting out of demons (3:1-8, 5:12-16, 14:8-10, 16:16-18). Prophecy was active throughout the period (13:2; Agabus, 11:28, 21:10-11; Philip's daughters, 21:9). Clearly, such gifts were not limited to the Day of Pentecost.

First Corinthians illustrates such gifts still being in operation. Paul enumerates them thus: "word of wisdom," "word of knowledge," "faith," "gifts of healings," "workings of powers" (miracles), "prophecy," "distinguishing of spirits," "kinds of tongues," and "interpretation of tongues" (12:8-10). The purpose of these gifts is, first, to edify the whole assembly of believers (esp. prophecy, *cf.* 14:3, 5, 12, 19, 31), and secondly, for personal edification (especially tongues, 14:4, 14, 15, 18). The nature of the gifts is spiritual, not natural: they are "manifestations of the Spirit" (v. 7), not the product of natural talent. They are not possible by natural means.

Having engaged in an overview of the subject, it is now possible to proceed with a study of the anti-Pentecostal arguments.

Anti-Pentecostal Allegations

Many of the anti-Pentecostal claims are based upon the same few basic points. However, one should note inconsistencies, instances in which commentators draw differing conclusions from the same evidence, and follow entirely divergent lines of reasoning.

First Allegation:
The Corinthian Tongues Were Not Genuine

One of the most basic arguments stems from the premise that the tongues mentioned in 1 Corinthians 12-14 were not genuine. Paul disapproved of the practice, it is presumed, and hoped to channel the church's attentions into other areas without expressly forbidding the use of tongues.[4] One wonders why he should do so. As an apostle, Paul is not afraid to forbid other actions on his own authority (*cf.* 14:34, I Thessalonians 4:11, II Thessalonians 3:30). Critics look to Chapter 13, wherein love, the "more excellent way," is elevated above spiritual gifts; and such verses as 14:19, wherein Paul states, "In the church I would rather speak five words with understanding . . . than ten thousand words in a tongue." Meanwhile, they minimize attention to passages such as, "I wish you all spoke in tongues" (14:5), "I shall pray with the Spirit and I shall pray with the mind also" (14:15), and "I thank God I speak in tongues more than all of you" (14:18).[5]

Many scholars see the Corinthian tongues as an illegitimate attempt to mimic the tongues of Pentecost. They point back to pre-Christian records of "dark sayings" and mysterious tongues in various cults.[6] The use of "magic words" and mystery languages by hucksters through the ages is an historical fact, and demonic activity cannot be ruled out. But Acts records genuine tongues being practiced as late as 19:6, after Paul's first visit to Corinth; and if the Corinthian tongues were spurious, would it not have been well within the character of Paul to utterly denounce its practitioners as he did the false teachers in 2 Corinthians 11:1-15?

Anti-Pentecostals often refer to tongues experiences as "ecstatic utterances."[7] This lends to them the connotation of a heightened emotional state, *i.e.,* a frenzy. In this out-of-control state, perhaps induced by shouting, shaking, running, jumping, loud music, etc., a person is likely to do anything. The "language" produced is simply "gibberish." This experience, they say, can happen to anybody, however sincere and well-meaning.[8] Dr. Charles Smith remarks,

> All the evidence suggests that biblical tongues were in all cases ecstatic utterances and essentially unintelligible. Any such utterances (today as well) may occasionally have included foreign words or phrases, but these were only bits and pieces in the mass of unrecognizable sounds.[9]

This, however, puts the tongues at Pentecost in the category of "gibberish," as well. How then, one might ask, did the witnesses "hear them in [their] own tongues speaking the greatness of God" (Acts 2:11)? Few commentators presume to label the Acts 2 episode as gibberish. Rather, many attempt to draw a line between the Acts experience and that at Corinth: the tongues at Jerusalem were real languages that could be understood (*i.e., xenolalia* or *xenoglossae*), while at Corinth "interpretation" was necessary. According to Dr. Carl Tuland,

> And the verb meaning to interpret [*hermeneuein*] is what is used in First Corinthians 12:10; 14:13, 26, and 28, a clear sign that the speaking in tongues at Corinth was not the natural talent or the charismatic gift of speaking *foreign* languages, for which no translation was required. The tongues-speaking in Corinth was ecstatic utterance or babbling. To be understood by others it had to be interpreted, but not translated.[10]

Moreover, John MacArthur notes further differences between the two passages.[11] Dr. Tuland's claim, however, is ably fielded by H. M. Ervin:

> As for Dr. Tuland's New Testament exegesis, a comparison of *methermeneuo* ["translate"] with *hermeneuo* shows that they are used interchangeably . . . .

> The confusion . . . is further compounded by his statement that "the verb meaning to interpret is what is used in First Corinthians 12:10; 14:13, 26, and 28." Actually, this verb is not used in any of these places. In First Corinthians 14:5, 13, 27 a third verb, *diermeneuo*, is used, while its cognate noun occurs in 14:28. In Luke 24:27 this verb means "to interpret," while in Acts 9:36 it means "to translate" . . . there is no exegetical support for his view that tongues in First Corinthians 14 are "ecstatic utterance or babbling."[12]

Furthermore, even a skeptic, S. Lewis Johnson, Jr., notes:

> It is well known that the terminology of Luke in Acts and of Paul in First Corinthians is the same. In spite of this some have contended for a difference between the gift as it occurred in Acts and as it occurred in Corinth. This is manifestly impossible from the standpoint of the terminology. This conclusion is strengthened when we remember

that Luke and Paul were constant companions and would have, no doubt, used the same terminology. . . .

. . . . it is most likely that the early believers used a fixed terminology in describing this gift, a terminology understood by them all.[13]

This issue, like so many others, cannot apparently be "proven" to everyone's satisfaction. Nevertheless, there is much evidence that casts the shadow of doubt on this particular line of reasoning.

Second Allegation:
The Gift of Tongues Ceased after the Apostolic Age

The major thrust of this argument is based on 1 Corinthians 13:8 and 10:

> . . . and whether prophecies [prophesyings], they shall be done away with; whether tongues, they shall cease; whether knowledge, it shall be done away with; but when the perfect [perfect thing, completion, fulfillment] comes [occurs, arrives, appears, comes into being], the partial shall be done away with.

In verse 8, prophecies and knowledge "shall be done away with" (katargethesetai, passive voice), but tongues "shall cease" (pausontai, middle voice). The significance of the middle voice in regard to tongues is, anti-Pentecostals state, that this means tongues will act upon themselves, i.e., cease without the action of the "perfect thing." According to John MacArthur,

> Prophecy and knowledge will be acted upon by some other force, and they will be done away. That other force Paul called "the perfect thing." It will cause prophecy and knowledge to cease while the gift of tongues will have ceased by itself before the perfect thing.

> The verb pauo tells us that tongues were to cease, meaning they would never start up again.[14]

These are broad assumptions, especially since the middle voice ending does not, in fact, bear temporal significance ("before the perfect thing"?). By MacArthur's rationale, tongues could just as well cease after the perfect thing. Moreover, the assertion that tongues shall cease without the action of the perfect thing contradicts the clear meaning of the text, which implies that it is the perfect thing that causes cessation in all three cases.

It is always dangerous to base theological stances on isolated occurrences of a particular word or verb ending—or, for that matter, on an isolated verse or verses. In its analysis of the middle voice, a standard Greek grammar states that "any analysis of the uses of the middle is of necessity more or less arbitrary. No rigid lines of distinction can in reality be drawn."[15] Concerning 1 Corinthians 13:8, D. A. Carson writes:

> . . . [*pauo*] regularly appears in middle form. In the active voice, its lexical meaning is "to stop, to cause to stop, to relieve"; in the middle, either "to stop oneself" (reflexive usage), or "to cease" (*i.e.*, it becomes equivalent to a deponent with intransitive force). It never unambiguously bears the meaning "to cease of itself" (*i.e.*, because of something intrinsic in the nature of the subject) . . . .[16]

The idea behind the anti-tongues interpretation is to prove that tongues-speaking as a legitimate spiritual gift passed away with the first-century Church. Many anti-Pentecostal scholars maintain a "dispensational" view here: tongues, along with some or all of the other "gifts," were for a sign, through which many would come to believe. After the "dispensation" was complete, and the Church was established, the signs were no longer needed, and ceased.[17]

There are mixed views of what "the perfect thing," which does away with the gifts, actually means.[18] It remains popular to interpret this as the New Testament canon—though there is no Biblical inference that such a single-volume canon is to be formed. The admonition not to "add" or "take away from the words of the book" in Revelation 22:18-19 properly refers to that single scroll (as was its original form); and the warning provides closure, serving as a "bookend" or mirror image to the blessing pronounced in 1:3. Therefore, it cannot justifiably be wielded as a weapon against any who would dare "add," as critics presume, to the overall mass of revelation by practicing charismatic gifts. This view also denies the possibility of a secondary level of personal or corporate revelation below that of inspired Scripture. Most Pentecostals are careful to subordinate all charismatic revelation to the teachings of Scripture, and not to literally "add" them to "the book." Many do not believe prophecies or interpretations should even be written down or recorded, lest they come to be considered equivalent to Scripture. Such revelation is for a particular person or a particular need, on an immediate basis, and not necessarily meant for universal declaration or preservation.

Many commentators look to the maturity of the Church as "the perfect thing." First Corinthians 13:11 is used to illustrate this: "When I was a child, I spoke as a child, thought as a child, reasoned as a child; when I became a man, I did away with the childish". The gifts, they say, were merely the springboard for the Church.[19] Essentially, they were just that. But was the Church indeed mature after the death of the Apostolic generation? When one explores the history of the early Church, one wonders if they had truly reached "maturity" by the time tongues were to cease; and indeed, whether we have yet to reach that point.

Now, however, even many non-Pentecostals come to the conclusion that "the perfect thing" refers to the Rapture or Second Coming of Christ. Stanley Toussaint writes that "the picture in verse 11 is not illustrating the church; rather it portrays the principle stated in verse 10," and continues, "First, the perfect thing mentioned in verse 10 best finds its meaning in the rapture. Second, verse 12, which explains verse 10, clearly refers to the coming of Christ for his own."[20] If the perfect thing is the Rapture or Christ's Second Coming, that implies that neither prophecy and knowledge, nor tongues, have yet been done away with. Moreover, Pentecostals assert that Pentecost inaugurated the Church Age (the Age of Grace, the Acceptable Year of the Lord, the age of the preaching of the Gospel, etc.), that the charismatic gifts were provided for this very time and purpose, and that they remain not only useful but necessary until the end of the age.

Finally, anti-Pentecostals point to a supposed void of spiritual gifts in the Church, particularly tongues, after the time of the apostles.[21] For instance, they adduce as evidence this excerpt from the commentary of John Chrysostom (c.347-407) on 1 Corinthians 12:1-11:

> This whole passage is exceedingly obscure; and what creates this obscurity is both ignorance in these matters and the cessation of things which happened then but do not now occur .... "Why indeed did they happen then, but do not happen any longer?"[22]

But one can also look to such references as Irenaeus (second century), "We hear many brethren in the church ... who through the Spirit speak all kinds of languages;"[23] and Justin Martyr (c.100-165), "For the prophetical gifts remain with us, even to the present time. And hence you ought to understand that [the gifts] formerly among [the Jews] have been transferred to us."[24]

"Prophetical gifts"—note the plural—probably includes tongues and interpretation, which also constitute messages from God.

It is a matter of opinion which references are more reliable. One thing that must be kept in mind is that, by the time of Chrysostom, the emphasis in the churches was upon the development of creeds in order to stem heresies, and upon catechetical training. The missionary zeal of the first century had faded; the character of the Church had changed.

The question remains whether those post-apostolic manifestations were, perhaps, erroneous. Eusebius (c.265-c.339) tells the story of Montanus who, speaking in demonic tongues and uttering false prophecy (in Eusebius' opinion), deceived some of the Phrygians.[25] Eusebius definitively labels many of the utterances as anti-Christ, thus failing the scriptural tests of prophecy (*cf.* 1 Corinthians 12:3, 1 John 4:1-3.). However, from these episodes and scant references alone, one cannot assume that all manifestations were, therefore, spurious. Modern scholars are ill-equipped to make a satisfactory examination of the phenomena, due to lack of evidence. If one follows the New Testament model, each prophetic message is to be judged by its content and character (1 Corinthians 14:29).

Third Allegation:
Tongues and Interpretation are Inferior Gifts

To the anti-Pentecostal, whether true tongues exist today or not, Paul certainly makes it clear that this is a lowly gift, hardly worth having.[26] After all, Paul puts it at the bottom of his lists (1 Corinthians 12:8-10, 28), declares it to be worthless without love (chapter 13), and explains its inferiority to prophecy (14:1-33).

However, simply by listing tongues and interpretation as spiritual gifts, Paul immediately elevates them above all human talents, abilities, wisdom, etc. Ministry without love, whether by tongues or other gifts, is worthless—yet love, too, is for now imperfect, being subject to the limitations of the present world. Ungifted man cannot love perfectly. What is the Christian to do until "the perfect thing" comes? He must let the Holy Spirit work through him. Love is, after all, not a gift of the Spirit but a fruit (Gal. 5:22-23, 2 Peter 1:3-9), and is "grown" in the one who allows the Spirit to work in and through him—one might presume by allowing spiritual gifts to flow through him. Spiritual gifts are intended to facilitate mighty works far beyond the limited capabilities of finite humanity.

Uninterpreted tongues are, clearly, inferior to prophecy—but when inter-preted, so that all can hear and understand the message from God, tongues become essentially equal to prophecy. As Paul writes, "Greater is he who prophesies than he who speaks in tongues, unless he interprets . . . ." (14:5).

Fourth Allegation: Modern "Tongues" are Fake

Regardless of whether tongues and interpretation passed away with the Apostles, many critics believe that today's manifestations are not genuine. They propose, variously, that manifestations may be "faked" in order to justify an attitude of spiritual superiority; that they can be "taught" and "learned"; that they can be psychologically induced upon a well-meaning person; or that they could be of demonic origin, designed to lead astray the unlearned and unsuspecting.[27] More generally, the popularity of tongues is attributed to a desire to escape the spiritual dryness of many traditional denominations, or to recapture the miraculous element found in the New Testament.[28] But Pentecostals themselves are quick to denounce mechanical methods and psychological inducements.[29]

Abuses have, indeed, occurred. But should these be allowed to cast a shadow upon all manifestations? Even Kenneth Gangel, a non-Pentecostal, proposes liberality: could not God, in his sovereignty, choose to outpour his Spirit at sundry times, in order to edify his Church, or as a sign to unbeliev-ers? Gangel calls for openmindedness.[30]

E. Lorna Kendall goes on to state that

> . . . the authenticity of tongue-speaking in the Christian
> community must be judged by its effects in the lives of those
> who practise (sic.) it, as, for example, in the mutual growth
> in the fruits of the Spirit, love, joy, peace, and the rest.
> Those who have received the gift, whether in answer to their
> own prayers or to the prayers of others, or whether it has
> come upon them without previous seeking, should be
> amongst those who are following what St. Paul called the
> better way, the way of love . . . .[31]

Perhaps Pentecostalism's effectiveness in this regard is attested by its pro-found expansion and growing acceptance with spiritually and emotionally hungry people around the world.

Conclusion

This study is not conclusive, but it was not intended as a proof that the gifts of tongues and interpretation as practiced today are genuine; indeed, how does one "prove" such a thing, any more than one can prove that Jesus Christ is risen? Such belief comes when the reality is experienced. Rather, this has been a study of the other side of the query: are the arguments against tongues valid?

In some instances, only questions have been raised. Elsewhere, the anti-tongues activists are called to account for dubious exegesis and slanted use of the evidence. They have been shown to be prejudicial in their use of "ec-static," as well as in their description of Paul's attitude toward tongues. Their exegesis of 1 Corinthians 13:8-10 has been shown to be much less clear-cut than they infer. Likewise, they have too quickly identified modern tongues with pagan religion and fakery, without offering concrete proof.

To the serious student of the Bible, such malpractices are disappointing at best. It bears upon every Christian to be a seeker of the truth from God's word, regardless of traditional views or personal prejudices. Whether the "tongues question" will ever be answered to the satisfaction of all remains a mystery. Yet, God is in control of the situation. As Christians, we can yet hope in the expectation of Christ's coming, when all things will be known, and we all shall be one.

Notes

1. Harold V. Synan, "The Pentecostal Movement in the United States" (Ph.D. dissertation, Univ. of Georgia, 1967), p. 179; and Frank J. Ewart, *The Phenomenon of Pentecost* (St. Louis: Pentecostal Publishing House, 1947), cited in William W. Menzies, *Anointed to Serve* (Springfield, MO: Gospel Publishing House, 1971), p. 72.

2. John MacArthur, Jr., *The Charismatics: A Doctrinal Perspective* (Grand Rapids: Zondervan, 1978) pp. 171-72.

3. D. A. Carson, *Exegetical Fallacies* (Grand Rapids: Baker, 1984), pp. 61-62.

4. See Chris W. Parnell, "What About Speaking in Tongues?" in *The New Wave of Pentecostalism* (Evangelical Foundation, Inc., 1973), pp. 35-36; W. M. Horn, "Speaking in Tongues: A Retrospective Appraisal," *Lutheran Quarterly* 17 (1965):325; F. W. Beare, "Speaking in Tongues," *Journal of Biblical Literature* 83 (1964):243.

5. See MacArthur, pp. 158, 162-66; Parnell, p. 35.

6. See Stuart D. Currie, "'Speaking in Tongues': Early Evidence Outside the New Testament Bearing on 'Glossais Lalein,'" *Interpretation* 19 (1965):285; E. Lorna Kendall, "Speaking with Tongues," *Church Quarterly Review* 168 (1967):12; MacArthur, p. 163; Parnell, p. 32.

7. Contrast H. M. Ervin, "As the Spirit Gives Utterance," *Christianity Today* 13 (1969):624.

8. See S. Lewis Johnson, Jr.. "A Symposium on the Tongues Movement: Introduction," *Bibliotheca Sacra* 120 (1963):225.

9. Dr. Charles Smith, *Tongues in Biblical Perspective* (BMH Books, n.d.), p. 40, cited in Kenneth O. Gangel, *Unwrap Your Spiritual Gifts* (Wheaton, Ill.: Victor Books, 1960), pp. 46-47.

10. Carl G. Tuland, "The Confusion About Tongues," *Christianity Today* 13 (1968):208.

11. See MacArthur, pp. 159-62.

12. Ervin, p. 626.

13. S. Lewis Johnson, "The Gift of Tongues and the Book of Acts," *Bibliotheca Sacra* 120 (1963):310, 311. *Cf.* Kendall, p. 14.

14. MacArthur, pp. 165, 169.

15. H. E. Dana and Julius R. Mantey, *A Manual Grammar of the Greek New Testament* (New York: Macmillan, 1927; rpt. ed. 1955).

16. Carson, pp. 78-79, cites examples of the New Testament use of *pausontai* in Luke 8:24, Acts 21:32.

17. Gangel, pp. 50-51, lists the comments of several anti-Pentecostals on this subject.

18. For a discussion of this question, see Stanley D. Toussaint, "First Corinthians Thirteen and the Tongues Question," *Bibliotheca Sacra* 120 (1963):312-15.

19. See MacArthur, pp. 74-75, 166-69.

20. Toussaint, p. 313.

21. See Currie, pp. 274-76; and Cleon L. Rogers, "The Gift of Tongues in the Post Apostolic Church (A.D. 100-400)" *Bibliotheca Sacra* 122 (1965):143.

22. Chrysostom *Homily* 29, cited in Currie, p. 276.

23. Irenaeus *Adversus Haereses* 5.6.1, cited in Rogers, p. 138.

24. Justin Martyr *Dialogue with Trypho* 82, cited in Rogers, p. 137.

25. Eusebius *Ecclesiastical History* 5.16.7-10, cited in Currie, p. 287.

26. See Parnell, pp. 35-36; Tuland, p. 209.

27. Parnell, p. 32; MacArthur, pp. 175-79; Horn, pp. 320-21.

28. Johnson, "Symposium," p. 225.

29. See Menzies, p. 127.

30. Gangel, pp. 50-51.

31. Kendall, p. 18.

Chapter 27.   A Pentecostal Education

A Short History of Higher Education in the Assemblies of God[*]

One of the original reasons for founding the Assemblies of God was in order to form its own distinctive educational institutions, along with funding foreign missions and establishing doctrinal standards.[1] However, the nature and purpose of these educational institutions has been the subject of some debate.

The development of Bible institutes seemed a natural for the young Assemblies of God, as an extension of the old short-term Bible schools upon which the Pentecostal Movement was founded. The institutes were private, incurring little state interference or control. But how much further should educational efforts in the Assemblies extend? Should training for secular careers be provided for those not called to preach? Should schools seek affiliation with accrediting agencies or any other groups? Should the Assemblies provide seminary-level instruction? These and other hard questions have faced the Assemblies of God throughout its history, and might continue to affect its course in the future.

Early Pentecostal Education

The Pentecostal revival began, for all essential purposes, at Bethel Bible School in Topeka, Kansas, in 1901. An outgrowth of the Holiness Movement, the Pentecostal Movement spread throughout much of the country within a few years. Vehicles such as the Azusa Street Mission, John Alexander Dowie's Zion City in Illinois, and various Pentecostal publications were instrumental in this spread. The new Pentecostal message fostered two important developments: first, the separation—reluctantly for most—of Pentecostals from established denominations. This, in turn, brought about the second development, the necessity of founding schools of their own that were distinctively Pentecostal.

The early Bible schools were generally informal and short-term, usually lasting four to six weeks.[2] When the course was done, the itinerant Bible

---

[*] Originally submitted to Dr. Edith Blumhofer, The Assemblies of God Theological Seminary, July 6, 1985.

teacher moved on. There were, however, some of longer duration, such as the Rochester Bible Training School (also known as Elim, actually begun before the Pentecostal outbreak), which operated from 1895 to 1924.[3] Some of the teachers of these small schools—T. K. Leonard, J. Roswell Flower, E. N. Bell, and P. C. Nelson, to name a few—were later to become leaders in the Assemblies of God.[4]

The emphasis of the early Pentecostal schools was on the training of ministers of all types: pastors, evangelists, missionaries, lay preachers, etc. The curriculum was pragmatic, and the main textbook was the Bible.

The Assemblies of God, formed in 1914, soon moved toward establishing more permanent schools in order to advance its cause. A number of Bible institutes were well established before World War II. Central Bible Institute, founded in 1922, remained the only General Council-operated school for many years. Other regional schools were operated by their respective districts, which the General Council has closely supervised over the years in order to ensure that pure Pentecostal doctrine is preached, and modernism and heresy discouraged. In 1925, CBI was chosen to serve as a model for all endorsed schools.[5]

The Bible institutes offered three-year programs. Students were instructed in Bible, preaching, missions, and related areas. They received first-hand ministry experience by evangelizing, performing Christian service, and conducting actual worship services. Practical education was what these plain, stalwart first-generation Pentecostals wanted. According to Joseph R. Flower, son of J. Roswell Flower, "The feeling [was that] the coming of the Lord was too near to become involved in advanced education."[6]

However, as early as the 1920s, a need for education beyond the institute level began to be realized. This was an era in which many professions, notably public school teaching, were stiffening their requirements.[7] Many Pentecostal young people had no wish to train for ministry, and were being drawn to secular or non-Pentecostal Christian colleges. At the same time, ministers who sought advanced training beyond the institute level had no Pentecostal seminary to attend. The expansion of Assemblies of God education, however, involved the approval of the constituency. As G. Raymond Carlson remarked,

> Large numbers of AG people entertained a fear that emphasis on education could have a deteriorating effect on the spiritual life of the movement. Their thinking could be cap-

suled in four words—revival, organization, education, stagnation.[8]

Establishment of Senior Colleges

The first accredited senior college programs in the Assemblies of God came about as more a necessity than a choice. The concern was two-fold: the loss of impressionable young people to the philosophies of the world, and the threat that the Movement might suffer loss and even die with its first generation.

As early as the 1929 General Council, a committee chaired by P. C. Nelson recommended the foundation of "an institution of college grade, where the most complete and thorough education can be obtained under Pentecostal auspices."[9] In time, several district schools expanded their programs to four years. Southwestern Bible Institute began providing a general education program at the junior college level in 1944.[10]

Still, a need was seen for a true liberal arts program. A liberal arts institution is designed to prepare young persons for a wide variety of careers, as well as graduate studies, by providing the broadest education possible. Betty Chase has pointed out that a liberal education is considered preferable for those who intend to go to seminary after college.[11]

A liberal arts college began to be seriously discussed by 1945.[12] At the 1947 General Council, the Education Committee reported that "many are being influenced by the insidiousness of modern education and others by the persistent repudiation of our particular doctrine, and they are lost to our ranks." Furthermore, the report reads,

> It is the feeling of your committee that these young people are too valuable for us to let slip through our fingers and that we are handicapping our progress by the loss of these potential lay-leaders in our churches.[13]

Even the proponents of higher education were reluctant to set aside the necessary finances. The main thrust of the Movement had always been evangelism, and evangelism brings to mind missions and literature, not liberal education. Foreign missions and the publishing enterprise received the lion's share of contributions and general funds. No funds were set aside for general education,[14] and the fear of overextension was very real.

Nevertheless, the following resolution was put before the 1953 General Council:

> WHEREAS, There is a great army of full gospel believing youth in our ranks
>
> AND WHEREAS, They are entitled to and are pursuing courses of higher education in college outside our Christian confession,
>
> AND WHEREAS, Many of them are being lost to our cause forever because of the philosophies, etc., with which they become indoctrinated . . .
>
> THEREFORE BE IT RESOLVED, That this General Council in session authorize the setting up of a SENIOR COLLEGE PROGRAM . . . .[15]

The resolution passed. A former military hospital in Springfield, Missouri, was secured as a campus for one dollar, and Evangel College opened its doors in 1955.

Founding a Pentecostal Seminary

Higher education has met with limited enthusiasm from large segments of the Assemblies of God constituency. This has been especially so in regard to starting a seminary, with fears of creeping formalism and modernism replacing the simple faith in the power of God upon which the Pentecostal Movement was established. This fear was not entirely unfounded: Darwinism, the influence of the Tubingen School of liberal Bible scholarship, Albert Schweitzer's work on the "historical Jesus," the Documentary Hypothesis ("JEDP"), Source Criticism, and the "demythologizing" of the Gospels by Rudolf Bultmann were just a few of the influences which had been destructive to Biblical authority and faith in other denominations.

Yet, one must wonder to what extent the founding fathers of the Movement dreamed of establishing a truly Pentecostal seminary. Many of them were highly educated men who went on to be staunch supporters of education in the Assemblies of God. E. N. Bell had attended Stetson University, Baptist Seminary in Louisville, and the University of Chicago Divinity School. P. C. Nelson, a native of Denmark, attended Rochester Theological Seminary. It was said that he could speak most European languages, and he translated Eric Lund's great book on hermeneutics from the Spanish.[16] Myer Pearlman was taught in Hebrew schools in his native England, and was fluent in Hebrew, Greek, Spanish, French, and Italian.[17]   Such men had observed both the dangers and the advantages of education, and in many cases considered it worth the risk.

Beginning in 1945, the bylaws of the Assemblies of God began to contain this statement:

> As progress and growth demand, the Educational *(sic.)* Department may provide a Full Theological Seminary Course in addition to the Bible Institute course, and provide post-graduate work for the graduates who seek special training for the ministry in the United States and foreign lands.[18]

Wishing to exert more control over the situation, the 1955 General Council voted to amend this statement, taking the decision out of the hands of the Education Department and making it subject to a vote of the general assembly.[19]   Nevertheless, Education Committee reports continued to be fully as alarming as had been those calling for the establishment of a liberal arts college. According to the 1957 General Council minutes,

> The report also called attention to a survey which indicated that one hundred and thirteen (113) students are presently enrolled in seminaries of non-Pentecostal denominations, furthering their education. Other studies indicated that many Assemblies of God high school and college students are planning to attend seminaries for training in graduate theology, and this knowledge points up a problem in our ranks which may become acute in the not too distant future.[20]

The need for chaplains for the military was especially pressing. It has been well within the purposes of the Assemblies of God to provide chaplains for the military; but as a rule, the armed services have required that every chaplain possess a minimum of graduate seminary training.   Although concessions were made for the Assemblies during World War II, it was only reasonable to expect all chaplains to work toward fulfilling this minimal requirement.[21]

Various preliminary studies were conducted, notably in 1956 and 1958. The 1958 study called attention to the growing demand for seminary studies, the need for Pentecostal chaplains and Bible college teachers, the fact that many Assemblies of God students were attending non-Pentecostal seminaries, and that some seminaries were ceasing to admit Pentecostals.[22] A further study was commissioned in 1961 to examine the feasibility of a seminary, with complete plans to be presented by 1967.[23]

Eventually, the establishment of a seminary was approved. In 1971, facilities for the school were included in the plans for the new International Distribution Center addition to the Assemblies of God headquarters building in Springfield, Missouri. Officially described as "a graduate school of theology and missions, providing advanced training beyond the baccalaureate level for ministers, missionaries, evangelists, and other Christian workers for effectual service at home and abroad,"[24] the Assemblies of God Graduate School (now the Assemblies of God Theological Seminary) opened its doors in the Fall of 1973.

Support of Assemblies of God Schools

Once the establishment of educational institutions was approved, a commitment to support those institutions became necessary. Such commitment was not lacking among Assemblies of God leaders. When the military requested leasing the Central Bible Institute campus for convalescent hospital facilities in 1943, the General Presbytery declined. They believed that "the interests of our country as well as of our constituency can be more largely served by continuing the Institution in its present status as a training center for ministers and missionaries, thus contributing to the up-building and maintenance of national morale."[25]

However, this commitment was by no means universal. A 1957 committee proposed that five percent of undesignated missions contributions go to support the Bible schools. The resolution failed to pass.[25] A 1959 report was quite insistent:

> Your committee feels that it is high time our movement is awakened to realize it MUST SUPPORT our schools as a necessary part of our great over-all work. We should realize that 90% of our entire foreign missionary staff received their training in our own Pentecostal schools and they have gone forth to establish 61 Bible schools .... Our future missionary staff, to say nothing of our great home-field depends upon our movement underwriting our educational program.[27]

The committee went on to recommend that each church give a sum proportionate to two dollars per member, and each district contribute 5 to 15 percent of its income to education, plus helping provide scholarships and endowments.[28]

Summary

The Assemblies of God educational system, along with hopes for its future, can best be summarized in the words of longtime General Superintendent Thomas F. Zimmerman:

> Education in itself will not convert the world. We must have the right kind of educators and the right kind of education. Evangelism is not enhanced with ignorance. We need to present to God our best. The greatest safeguard that we can have is to shore up our training programs and support our schools, so that we can erect the kind of guidelines we expect our educational programs to have. I believe we have a responsible and responsive educational program, and I want to see it kept that way.[29]

Notes

1. J. Roswell Flower, quoted in Irwin Winehouse, *The Assemblies of God, A Popular Survey* (NY: Vantage Press, 1959), p. 171.

2. Kenneth O. Gangel, *Christian Education: Its History and Philosophy* (Chicago: Moody Press, 1983), p. 140. On of Luther's well-known sermons was entitled, "The duty of Sending Children to School."

3. Gleason L. Archer, Jr., *A Survey of Old Testament Introduction*, rev. ed. (Chicago: Moody Press, 1974), pp. 83-169. *Cf.* Gerhard Hasel, *Old Testament Theology*, 3d ed. (Grand Rapids: Wm. B. Eerdmans Publishing Company, 1972), pp. 23-31.

4. Archer, pp. 302-384.

5. Robert M. Grant and David Tracy, *A Short History of the Interpretation of the Bible*, 2d ed. (Phila.: Fortress Press, 1973), pp. 110-118. *Cf.* Everett F. Harrison, *Introduction to the New Testament* (Grand Rapids: Wm. B. Eerdmans, 1971), pp. 137-234.

6. William W. Menzies, *Anointed to Serve* (Springfield, MO: Gospel Publishing House, 1971), pp. 34-40.

7. Don P. Gray, "A Critical Analysis of the Academic Evolutionary Development within the Assemblies of God Higher Education Movement, 1914-1974" (D.Ed. Thesis, Southwestern Baptist Theological Seminary, 1976), p. 22.

8. Gray, p. 21.

9. Gray, pp. 20-22, 26.

10. Charlotte Luckey, "History and Development of Assemblies of God Education," *Assemblies of God Educator* 10 (Nov.-Dec. 1965):4-5. Cr. Donald F. Johns, "A Philosophy of Religious Education for the Assemblies of God" (Ph.D. dissertation, New York University, 1962), p. 19.

11. Joseph R. Flower, personal letter to Carolyn D. Baker, Springfield, Missouri, Nov. 15, 1983, appended to Carolyn D. Baker, "The Stunted Growth of the Assemblies of God Formal Education Between 1914 and 1973 with Reasons and Suggestions for Future Leaders and Educators" (term paper, Assemblies of God Graduate School, 1983), in the Assemblies of God Archives, Springfield, MO.

12. Minutes of the General Council, September 4-9, 1947, Grand Rapids, MI, in the Assemblies of God Archives, Springfield, MO, pp. 16-18.

13. G. Raymond Carlson, personal letter to Carolyn Baker, Oct. 12, 1983, cited in Baker, pp. 4-5.

14. Menzies, p. 362.

15. Menzies, pp. 359, 366. Winehouse, p. 174.

16. Minutes of the General Council, September 20-26, 1929, no place (in the Assemblies of God Archives), p. 83.

17. Menzies, p. 359.

18. Betty Chase, "The Pentecostal Pardox" *Assemblies of God Educator* 3 (Sept.-Oct. 1958):4.

19. Minutes of the General Council, September 13-18, 1945, Springfield, MO (in the Assemblies of God Archives), p. 17.

20. Minutes of the General Council, 1947, p. 17.

21. Hardy Steinberg, personal letter to Carolyn Baker, Oct. 13, 1983, Springfield, MO, appended to Baker, "Stunted Growth."

22. Minutes of the General Council, August 26-September 2, 1953, Milwaukee, WI (in the Assemblies of God Archives), p. 30.

23. Minutes of the General Council, 1945, p. 25.

24. Minutes of the General Council, September 1-6, 1955, Oklahoma City, OK (in the Assemblies of God Archives), p. 43.

25. An excellent example of anti-higher education voting is found in the 1947 Minutes, p. 22, concerning the establishment of a liberal arts college. The vote was 326 for, 641 against.

26. Minutes of the General Council, August 28-September 3, 1957, Cleveland, OH (in the Assemblies of God Archives), pp. 50-51.

27. Minutes of the General Council, August 29-September 1, 1959, San Antonio, TX (in the Assemblies of God Archives), p. 84.

28. Minutes of the General Council, August 25-30, 1965, Des Moines, IA (in the Assemblies of God Archives), p. 68.

29. Minutes of the General Council, August 14-19, 1975, Denver, CO (in the Assemblies of God Archives), p. 147.

30. Minutes of the General Council, September 2-7, 1943, Springfield, MO (in the Assemblies of God Archives), p. 7.

31. Minutes of the General Council, 1957, p. 51.

32. Minutes of the General Council, 1959, p. 83.

33. *Ibid.*, pp. 83-84.

34. Minutes of the General Council, August 11-16, 1983, Anaheim, CA (in the Assemblies of God Archives), p. 57.

Appendices

Appendix 1.   Fields White Unto Harvest*

Note: The following is a review of the book, *Fields White Unto Harvest: Charles F. Parham and the Missionary Origins of Pentecostalism* by James R. Goff, Jr. (Fayetteville, Arkansas: University of Arkansas, 1988).

Charles F. Parham is best known as the leader of the Bethel Bible School in Topeka, Kansas, at the time of the Pentecostal outbreak in 1901. Few major works have been written on Parham's life since Charles Shumway's scathing Boston University dissertation, "A Critical History of Glossolalia," was published in 1919. Shumway maintained that "tongues-speaking" was a mere psychological phenomenon which appealed to individuals lacking spiritual understanding.

Born to respectable Kansas farmers in 1873, the capable, well-read, and charismatic young Parham rose to national attention as the recognized leader of the Apostolic Faith movement, only to fall from grace a few years later in the wake of a sex scandal. Fields White Unto Harvest is by far the most objective and well-documented sourcebook available on Parham's life. Goff, though sympathetic with both Parham and Pentecostalism, believes that "faith is never helped by sentimental history."

Goff's intended objectivity, however, is noticeably uneven. His accounts of miraculous events often sound incredulous, perhaps a case of overcompensating. In contrast, Goff provides a lengthy defense of Parham over allegations of sexual misconduct. Based on hearsay evidence, Parham was arrested for alleged sodomy, then a felony in Texas. Apparently no charges were ever filed. Goff builds a strong case that Parham was in fact framed for the crime by Zion City (Illinois) leader Wilbur Voliva, the anti-Pentecostal who inherited John Alexander Dowie's considerable following. Nevertheless, rivals in and out of Pentecostal ranks, notably W. Faye Carothers of Texas, seem to have used the episode as an occasion to discredit Parham and destroy his influence.

Goff presents Parham as very much a product of his background. Affected by the uncertainty of frontier existence, sympathetic to the Populist cause, he longed for God's intervention, a longing supported by the apocalypticism, millennarianism, and evangelistic zeal of the Holiness Movement. Claiming

---

* Originally published in *Paraclete* 24 (Summer 1990):31-32.

healing from rheumatic fever at the age of 18, Parham aspired to lead others in the quest for divine healing. Here he was strongly influenced by the likes of Dowie, Frank W. Sandford, John Darby, and Benjamin H. Irwin.

Parham's contributions to Pentecostal theology have often been minimized. Rather than a shadowy figure on the fringes of the Topeka revival, Goff spotlights Parham as "Projector of the Apostolic Faith" and the catalyst of the movement. Although denied by Parham himself, Goff believes the young evangelist led the students of the Bethel Bible School toward an expected outcome, the Baptism in the Holy Spirit evidenced by speaking in tongues. Parham insisted the outpouring was a spontaneous move of God upon the entire student body.

Parham, claims Goff, was the first to identify a theological and functional link between speaking in tongues and the experience of Spirit baptism. Further, Parham defined the nature of tongues as *xenoglossae* (literally, "foreign tongues"), the God-given ability to speak a foreign language one has never learned. This ability, he thought, would enable Pentecostal believers to go forth as missionaries and evangelize the world within a short time. He made it a point to note that tongues had often been understood by foreigners and language experts in his meetings. Some well-meaning followers made earnest attempts at *glossography*, the writing of divine messages in cryptic scrawls.

Goff does not sidestep the more dubious elements of Parham's theology. Parham espoused the Anglo-Israel Theory (following Sandford) that the British, and by extension Anglo-Saxon Americans, were descended from the lost tribes of Israel. Raised in a segregated society, he welcomed black Americans to his meetings but felt they should be seated separately. William J. Seymour, the black Pentecostal whom Parham had sent forth from his Texas work, broke with Parham after the latter visited the Azusa Street work. Appalled by racial mixing and what he considered extreme emotionalism, Parham tried to establish his control but was rebuffed. He never gained real influence in Los Angeles.

Parham rejected the idea of eternal punishment, opting for a "Conditional Immortality." Only the righteous, he said, were granted eternal existence. Spirit-baptized Christians would form a special elite, the Bride of Christ who, after evangelizing the world, would rule with Christ in the Millennium. Parham and his followers expected the Second Coming by 1925.

Goff's book is well-researched and thoroughly documented. He treats the often neglected Pentecostal Movement in the Houston, Texas, area prior to

Azusa Street, as well as the works in Kansas, Missouri, and Zion City. The book includes three short appendices, a helpful but incomplete index, and a generous bibliography. The book is well edited (though Texans will notice a few errors in geographical and historical detail). Goff might have made special note that Pentecostal scholar and author Edith Waldvogel is one and the same with Edith Blumhofer [both of which names he mentions].

The story of Charles Parham shows us what great things God can do with earnest seekers who always want more of God. In delicate balance, Goff admits to us that earnest Christians such as Parham, in their zeal for the things of God, sometimes stray into incorrect doctrine and unprofitable speculations. This should remind us that zeal alone will not lead us to the truth.

Appendix 2.   Gospel of the Ascension[*]

Note: The following is a review of *The Gospel of the Ascension: Good News from Within the Veil!* by Delmer R. Guynes (Kuala Lumpur, Malaysia: Calvary Church Press, 1986).

Books published over 5 years ago are seldom the subject of a review. But some books are an exception. After leaving his position as president of Southwestern Assemblies of God College (to which he later returned), Delmer Guynes entered into an international preaching/teaching ministry he called the Institute of Ascension Ministry. With his wife Eleanor, who is also qualified, he produced several volumes as texts for that ministry. These include *The Apostolic Nature of the Church*; *The Transformed Ministry*; *The Human Side of the Ministry*; *In Search of Philadelphia: a Church With Throne Room Ministry*; and the present volume. In addition, Eleanor Guynes authored *How To Live Like a Queen*. Published in Malaysia, these books were not widely distributed in the United States.

Guynes has always had a missionary heart. About 1970, God began to birth in him a vision for the release of ministry gifts around the world. This was climaxed in a literal "mountaintop experience." While climbing up Jardine's Lookout, a peak overlooking Hong Kong, ". . . suddenly a wind from heaven simply surged through my whole being. I was totally liberated by the Spirit, and exultant in the flow of the Holy Spirit through my life as I felt the great Head of the Church bestowing His ministry gifts and graces upon choice servants in China, Japan, India, Africa, America, and other parts of the world. . . . I remember especially looking northward towards the vastness of China . . . and sensing that Jesus was raising up and endowing apostles, prophets, evangelists, pastors, and teachers for the exploding church there" (p. 13).

Nevertheless, Guynes does not base his case upon personal revelation; he tries to ground it solidly in Scripture. *The Gospel of the Ascension* is part of a grand quest for an accurate Biblical perspective and emphasis on the present position of the Church, the relationship of the present-day church to that position, and what Christ wants to do through His church through His grace-gifts (*charismata*).

---

[*] Originally published in *Paraclete* 26 (Fall 1992):29

One might argue that the Ascension and Exaltation of Christ (which Guynes takes together under the rubric "Ascension ministry") represent the two great, unplumbed doctrines of the Church, which should rank alongside the Incarnation and the Atonement. The Ascension and Exaltation refer to the spiritual work of Jesus beginning with His resurrection (or with His death on the cross, in the view of some). This work was promised in John 14-17, inaugurated at Pentecost, and continues in the bestowal of spiritual gifts and gifted leaders upon the Church for power and edification (see Ephesians 4:7-16).

The vitality of this subject for Pentecostals is evident. Many Pentecostals know the Giver and observe the gifts but understand little about the giving process or its purposes. Guynes sees true charismatic ministry today "being stymied by various kinds of humanistic and self-projecting activities" (p. 11). He deprecates professionalism and self-based so-called ministry alike (p. 148). True ministry exalts not the earthen vessel but the exalted Christ.

The underlying theme of the book seems to be that Christians need to understand the spiritual work Christ has done and continues to do, and how He wishes to work through His people. The implication is that Christians need to move themselves into the flow of ministry grace in order to know God's will and to be used of God; the alternative is spiritual poverty. Chapter titles include, "The Ascension Through the Bible," "The Exalted Christ and the Gift of the Holy Spirit," "The Greater Works of the Ascended Christ," "Jesus Exalted, Head Over All Things to the Church," and "The Exalted Jesus, Head of the New Creation."

This book is highly valuable, though seminal. Guynes is a visionary. His work is not the last word. But he has contributed an important work on a vital subject to what will hopefully be an ongoing process of discovery.

Appendix 3.   Gifts of the Spirit in 1 Corinthians 12

Insights from Pentecostal Scholars

The following constitutes my notes on spiritual gifts taken from various Pentecostal authors.

1. The Word of Wisdom

- Stanley Horton[1]

    - Scriptural insight and practical application of God's Word. Divine counsel. The right application of knowledge (p. 271).

    - Corporate: for a group worship context. For the edification of the local church. For an immediate need or for some particular occasion.

    - Immediate and occasional: for an immediate need or for some particular occasion. Only enough information is revealed to meet the immediate need.

    - Not resident: not an endowment of wisdom to a person, but a single message to meet a particular need.

- Harold Horton[2]

    - "The supernatural revelation . . . of Divine Purpose . . . of the Mind and Will of God . . . of His Plans and Purposes . . . (p. 56).

    - The purpose of God for the future (like John's revelation on Patmos) (pp. 57, 164). See Numbers 12:6.

    - Not natural wisdom enhanced or developed (p. 164).

    - Purposes:

    - "To warn an individual of approaching danger" (Paul at Malta) (p. 64f.).

---

[1]   Stanley Horton, *What the Bible Says About the Holy Spirit* (Springfield, MO: Gospel Publishing House).

[2]   Harold Horton, *The Gifts of the Spirit* (Springfield, MO: Gospel Publishing House, 1934).

- ■ "To make known or confirm a missionary call" (Macedonian call) (p. 65f.).

- ■ "To apprise of blessing or judgment to come" (p. 66).

- ■ "To reveal the future" (Agabus) (p. 67).

- ■ "To give personal guidance in a particular direction in special circumstances—not to supplement human judgment in ordinary circumstances" (pp. 67f.).

- • L. Thomas Holdcroft[1]

  - ■ Specific but limited insight on God's purpose (p. 146).

  - ■ Like legal advice: you get a 'word,' not full expertise.

2. The Word of Knowledge

- • Stanley Horton

  - ■ Closely related to the Word of Wisdom.

  - ■ "A declaration of gospel truth or the application of it." "Supernatural illumination of the gospel, especially in the ministry of teaching and preaching."

  - ■ The Holy Spirit is to "teach you all things" (John 14:26, 15:26, 16:13) (pp. 271ff.).

  - ■ "There is absolutely no indication in the Bible that the word of knowledge is meant to bring revelation of where to find lost articles or of what disease or sin a person may be suffering from. Rather, it gives deeper insight into the Scripture" (pp. 272f.).

  - ■ See Acts 10:47f., 15:7ff., 10:11ff., 34ff.

- • Harold Horton

  - ■ "The supernatural revelation by the Holy Spirit of certain facts in the mind of God" (p. 39).

  - ■ Not an endowment of knowledge dwelling within the person. "It is not a faculty but a revelation" (p. 40).

  - ■ Not one of the vocal gifts. Not an utterance, but can borrow the services of the gift prophecy (p. 41).

---

[1] L. Thomas Holdcroft, *The Holy Spirit: A Pentecostal Interpretation* (Springfield, MO: Gospel Publishing House, 1979).

- Examples: Samuel, Nathaniel, Ananias and Sapphira, the woman at the well (John 4). Horton gives an example of a woman at a bakery in Ireland.

- Purposes:

    1. Aids in effectual prayer for others in trouble (Burton, Frodsham examples) (p. 48).

    2. "Recover lost persons or property" (p. 49).

    3. "Reveal facts in private lives for spiritual correction or profit" (3 examples, F. B. Meyer).

- L. Thomas Holdcroft

    - Awareness of facts apart from the senses (p. 148).

    - Can be given by vision or angel (Acts 9:10ff., 27:23; 2 Cor 12:4).

    - Simeon, Luke 2:26; Woman at the well, John 4:17; Ananias and Sapphira, Acts 5; shipwreck, Acts 27:10.

- Frank Holder

    "By this means, secret sin has been exposed; causes of sickness sometimes revealed, and when matters are put right, healing has been given. Deliverances in times of danger have come through fervent prayer, when the presence of danger has been revealed to a person sometimes many thousands of miles away" (in Holdcroft, p.149f.).

3. The Discernings of Spirits

- Stanley Horton

    - The plural "discernings" indicates a variety of ways in which this gift may be manifest" (p. 276f.).

    - Possibly related to "judging" in 1 Cor 14:29. "Supernaturally given perception" (1 John 4:1). "Involves forming a judgment." Separates the voice of the Holy Spirit from human feelings, spiritual ignorance, excessive zeal.

    - "A specific gift for a specific occasion"—the gift is not resident in the individual.

    - Acts 5:3, 8:20ff., 13:10, 16:16ff.

- Harold Horton

  - Not "spiritual Thought-Reading" (p. 70). Not psychological insight. Separates between true and false prophets (pp. 71f.).

  - Purposes:

    1. To help deliver "afflicted, oppressed, tormented" (Mt 4:24)(p. 74).

    2. To "discover a servant of the devil" (Elymas, Acts 13:9)(p. 76).

    3. To ruin the plans of the devil (Acts 13:9).

    4. To expose seduction and error (1 Tim 4:1, 2 Peter 2:1).

    5. To unmask false miracle-workers (p. 77).

- L. Thomas Holdcroft

  - To "enable the believer to form judgments and recognize identities in the realm of the spirits" (p. 150). It "perceives basic underlying reality" (p. 150).

  - "Does not enable one to discern people" (p. 150). Example: the chariots of the angels revealed to Elisha's servant, 2 Kings 6:17) (p. 152).

4. Faith

- Stanley Horton

  - Not saving faith or faithfulness (as in "faith" the Fruit of the Spirit, Galatians 5:22f.)(p. 273).

  - Corporate: to raise the level of faith in the Body through edification.

- Harold Horton

  - "The Gift of Faith is a supernatural endowment by the Spirit whereby that which is uttered or desired by man or spoken by God, shall eventually come to pass" (pp. 121f.). Produces other miracles.

  - "Miracle-utterance," "miracle-assurance" (p. 122).

  - A subtle gift (p. 129). "The Workings of Miracles works miracles, while the Gift of Faith trusts for miracles" (p. 128).

- Miracle—an act; faith—a process.

- Not saving faith or natural faith (p. 119). Not faith the fruit. "Faith the fruit comes after salvation; Faith the Gift comes after the Baptism in the Holy Spirit" (p. 121). "Faith the fruit is for character; faith the Gift is for power" (p. 120).

- L. Thomas Holdcroft

  - Given selectively (p. 156).

  - Not faith in faith itself, but in God (157).

- Weymouth

  - "Special faith" (in Holdcroft, p.156).

5. The Workings of Miracles (Powers)

- Stanley Horton

  - Plural—many varieties or deeds available.

  - "Direct, divine interventions."

  - Not primarily nature miracles (Donald Gee).

  - Demonstrate Jesus as Victor (p. 275).

  - A foretaste of immortality.

- Harold Horton

  - Purposes:

    1. Miraculous deliverance (p. 110).

    2. To provide for needs (pp. 111f.).

    3. To carry out divine judgments (pp. 113f. [see story]).

    4. To confirm the Word (p. 114).

    5. To deliver from danger.

    6. To raise the dead.

    7. To glorify God.

- L. Thomas Holdcroft

  - "Works of supernatural power or deeds of might rather than marvels or signs" (p. 158). Transcends nature.

  - Purposes:

    1. To provide for special needs.

    2. To confirm the Gospel witness (Acts 3:1-16, 8:39f., 16:25ff. 20:9ff., 28:8-10).

    3. To bestow judgment (Acts 5:1ff., 13:7ff.).

    4. Exorcism (Acts 13:7ff., 19:11f.).

6. The Gifts of Healings

- Stanley Horton

  - Plural. Some say:

    1. a variety of forms

    2. different gifts healed by different people

    3. a supply of healings given to a given individual to dispense (p. 273)

  - "Every healing is a special gift . . . for the sick person . . . . the Spirit does not make men healers" (p. 274).

  - "Gifts of healings are available to every member of the Body to minister to the sick" (p. 275).

  - Not a "resident power."

- Harold Horton

  - The plural means many gifts.

  - Specific to certain diseases (?).

  - Embodied in the individual (?) (p. 103).

  - Healing by anointing is not by gifts of healings but "in response to obedience and in answer to believing prayer" (?) (p. 103).

  - Sinners are more readily healed than saints (as a witness) (p. 104).

  - Purposes:

1. To deliver the sick and destroy works of the devil (p. 99).

2. To establish the Gospel message (p. 100).

3. To establish Jesus' claims (p. 100).

4. To establish the Resurrection of Jesus (p. 101).

5. To draw people to the Gospel (p. 101).

6. To turn people to God.

7. To convince unbelievers (p. 102).

8. To Glorify God.

9. To inspire faith and courage.

- L. Thomas Holdcroft

  - "An assortment of individual healing portions to those who need them."

  - "The gift of the gift of healings" (p. 153).

  - "Divine charity" (p. 154).

  - "A package of healing remedies to be shared as gifts with others."

  - Like tongues, it is given on a "twofold basis": to the individual (1 Cor. 12:7) and to the church (12:28).

  - Unbelievers as well as believers may be healed.

  - They are "primarily a sign" (p. 155).

  - "To equip the Church and its workers with the credentials needed to fulfill the Great Commission" (p. 154).

  - Healing of believers is a covenant blessing; healing of unbelievers ratifies God's servant (p. 155).

- Eldin R. Corsie

  - "Every healing is a special gift. There are no healers" (in Holdcroft, p. 153).

7. Kinds of Tongues

- Stanley Horton

    - To Paul, "mysteries" always means spiritual truth (1 Cor. 14:2) (p. 278).

    - Our spirit is the medium through which the gift operates.

    - Yielding is necessary.

    - Interpretation is necessary for edification.

    - No gift is unimportant.

    - "Everyone should have something to contribute" (p. 231).

    - Responsibility for order and regulation of gifts not on the elders but on each individual (p. 234).

    - Purposes:

        1. A judgment sign (see Isaiah 28:11). "A sign to the unbeliever, making him realize he is separated from God and cannot understand God's message" (p. 229).

        2. To draw attention.

        3. A sign of supernatural power.

- G. Raymond Carlson

    - "The gifts or manifestations listed in 1 Corinthians 12 operate through any Spirit-led believer to accomplish the work of the Spirit in a specific situation" (in *Paraclete*, Summer 1991).

- Harold Horton

    - The least of the gifts (p. 146).

    - Not for guidance or direction in personal matters, but for edification, exhortation, and comfort (p. 145).

    - Corporate context only—private groups cause mischief.

    - The Word of God is for guidance.

    - Tongues and Interpretation should be reserved for "believer's meetings."

    - Purposes:

        1. Evidence of Baptism in the Holy Spirit (p. 133).

    2.   To speak supernaturally to God (p. 134).

    3.   To magnify God (Acts 10:46).

    4.   To edify ourselves.

    5.   So "our sprits distinct from our understanding might pray" (p. 136).

    6.   With Interpretation, to edify the Church.

    7.   As a sign to unbelievers.

    8.   For our profit.

- L. Thomas Holdcroft

  - Not a means of preaching in foreign languages (p. 164).

  - The only difference between the sign of Baptism and the gift is one of function (p. 161).

  - "The mind is primarily a spectator to the events, and it neither frames the utterances, nor does it premeditate or prearrange them" (p. 161).

  - "The regulations impose no real bondage, and casting them away provides no real liberty" (p. 164).

  - Purposes:

    1.   A medium for prayer and worship (1 Cor. 14:2, 14f.; Rom. 8) (p. 162).

    2.   A medium for edification (1 Cor. 14:4f., 18; Acts 2:11).

    3.   A sign (1 Cor. 14:22, Isaiah 28:9ff.) (p. 163).

8. Interpretation of Tongues

- Stanley Horton

  - "The giving of the meaning of essential content of the utterance in tongues" (p. 278). See Jn. 1:42, 9:7; Heb. 7:2.

  - Direct from the Holy Spirit, not an ability resident in the individual.

  - Can come "by vision, by burden, or by suggestion" (Donald Gee).

- A step of faith required: the Holy Spirit may give only the first few words to start with (p. 279).

- The content may include revelation, knowledge, prophesying (exhortation), doctrine (teaching) (p. 226).

- Tongues, with interpretation, brings edification just like prophecy (1 Cor. 14:5).

- L. Thomas Holdcroft

  - Includes exposition and application (p. 165).

  - Tongues and Interpretation may have the equivalent result as prophecy (p. 166f.).

  - Can be in the first person (Acts 13:2).

- Harold Horton

  - A "declaration of the meaning" (p. 149). "May be pictorial, parabolic, descriptive or literal" (p. 149).

  - Not from the mind of the interpreter (p. 147). Direct from God as are tongues (p. 148). Not translation (p. 149).

  - "The temperament, natural gifts and training, as well . . . as the nationality of the possessor of the Gift will influence the statement" (p. 151).

  - The same person need not always interpret (p. 153).

  - Not more than 3 tongues in a service (p. 154).

  - Requires more faith than tongues. Human error possible.

  - 1 Cor. 14:5 suggests Tongues and Interpretation are of the same value as prophecy (pp. 162, 172).

  - Tongues and Interpretation should be reserved for "believers' meetings."

- Robert C. Dalton

  - Interpretation of tongues is just as much a miracle as speaking in tongues (in Holdcroft, p. 165).

9. Prophecy

- Stanley Horton

  - Related to illumination of the mysteries of the Gospel.

  - Can be variety in its expression.

  - The Holy Spirit touches sensitive spots, reveals secrets, brings conviction, worship, encouragement. See Peter's sermon.

  - "Available to any member of the congregation" (p. 276). All encouraged by Paul to seek it.

  - Must be judged (p. 233).

  - "Must not be allowed to become a means of being blessed, and then doing nothing about it" (p. 233).

- Michael Harper

  - "It is not an ability given to someone to prophesy at will. It is a special anointing given at a selected moment by the Spirit for a distinct purpose" (in Holdcroft, p. 177).

- Stanley Horton

  - Related to illumination of the mysteries of the Gospel.

  - A variety in expression is possible.

  - The Holy Spirit touches sensitive spots, reveals secrets, brings conviction, worship, and encouragement.

  - "Available to any member of the congregation" (p. 276).

  - All are encouraged by Paul to seek it.

  - Must be judged (p. 233).

  - "Must not be allowed to become a means of being blessed, and then doing nothing about it" (p. 233).

  - Peter's sermon is an example.

- Harold Horton

  - Divinely inspired and anointed utterance. The most important gift of utterance (p. 159).

- ■ Not a sign of prophetic office: the office of Prophet is different than in the Old Testament. Additional gifts are necessary for that office, as well as a commission to leadership. The office are gifts of Jesus to his Church, but the gifts of the Holy Spirit are to individuals (pp. 160ff.). The New Testament prophet foretells, but never 'leads'" (p. 165).

- ■ Not necessarily predictive (see Word of Wisdom) (p. 163).

- ■ Can involve Word of Wisdom, Word of Knowledge (Acts 11:28, Lk. 1:48), Gift of Faith (Ezek. 37) (p. 164).

- ■ Does not replace or add to Word of God (p. 173).

- ■ Must be judged "by the other prophets present" (p. 173).

- ■ Prophecy and Interpretation are not for correction in the assembly (p. 169).

- ■ Can be colored or distorted by one's own thoughts (p. 174).

- ■ The gift is subject to the prophet.

- ■ "The sharper the tool, the more need for care in its employment" (p. 159).

- ■ Purposes:
  1. "Speaking to men supernaturally" (1 Cor. 14:3) (p. 167).
  2. "To edify the Church" (14:4) (p. 168).
  3. "To exhort the Church" (14:3) (p. 169).
  4. "To comfort the Church" (14:3, 31).
  5. To "learn" (14:31).
  6. "To convict the unbeliever and make manifest the secrets of his heart" (14:24f.) (p. 170).

- • L. Thomas Holdcroft
  - ■ Prophecy illuminates Scripture (p. 169).
  - ■ Prophecy does not have the authority of Scripture (p. 167).
  - ■ Prophecy is not a substitute for preaching Scripture (pp. 169f.).
  - ■ Not the same as Old Testament prophecy (p. 170).
  - ■ Can be written or acted out (Agabus, Acts 21:10f.).

- Purposes:
    1. Edifies (1 Cor. 14:3)—"prophetic speech is good building material."
    2. Exhorts (14:3).
    3. Comforts (14:3).
    4. Convicts (14:24) (p. 168).
    5. Communicates (14:31).
    6. Predicts (Acts 21:10) (p. 168).

- G. Raymond Carlson
    - Judging is not by prophets only, but by all. "The prophet's words—not the prophet himself—are judged" (in *Paraclete* 25, Summer 1991, p. 5).
    - The prophet can err without being false.
    - Prophecy does not interpret Scripture—it is judged *by* Scripture.
    - Church governance is not by prophetic pronouncements (pp. 5f.). Prophets are not leaders. Those who demand authority generally bring bondage.
    - "The gifts or manifestations listed in 1 Corinthians 12 operate through any Spirit-led and yielded believer to accomplish the work of the Spirit in a specific situation. The Spirit-energized ministries or callings mentioned in Ephesians 4 indicate a greater regularity of operation or manifestation so that the Body recognizes that the Spirit has indeed appointed and anointed persons with specialized callings" (p. 2).

Appendix 4. Comparison of Spiritual Gift Lists

Rom. 12:6-8	1 Cor. 12:8-10	1 Cor. 12:28	1 Cor. 12:29-30	1 Cor. 13:1-3, 8	Eph. 4:11
	Word of Wisdom			Understanding Mysteries	
	Word of Knowledge			Knowledge	
	Faith			Faith	
	Gifts of Healings	Gifts of Healings	Gifts of Healings*		
	Workings of Miracles	Miracles	Workers of Miracles*		
	Discernings of Spirits				
	Kinds of Tongues	Diversities of Tongues	Speakers in Tongues*	Speaking in Tongues	
	Interpretation of Tongues		Interpreters*		
Prophecy	Prophecy	(Prophets)*	(Prophets)*	Prophecy	(Prophets)*
Ministry		(Helps)*			
Teaching		Teachers*	Teachers*		(Pastors/Teachers)*
Exhortation	(Prophecy)#				(Pastors/Teachers)*@
Giving		(Helps)*		Giving	
Ruling		Governments*			
Mercy		Helps*		(Giving)	
		Apostles*	Apostles*		Apostles*
		Prophets*	Prophets*		Prophets*
					Evangelists*
					Pastors/Teachers*
			Martyrdom		

( ) Possible overlap into other gifts, or can be categorized in different ways.
* Principally refer to gifted persons who are then gifts of Christ to his Church.
# According to 1 Cor. 14:3, prophecy can include exhortation.
@ One of the principle tasks of pastors is exhortation.

Appendix 5.   Functions of the Gift of Tongues

There is one gift of tongues, but it has various uses or functions:

1. The initial evidence of the infilling or Baptism of the Holy Spirit.

    ■ Speaking in tongues is normative to the Baptism in the Holy Spirit, being included whenever outward manifestations are mentioned (Acts 2:4, 16-18, 33, 38-39; 10:44-46; 11:15; 19:2, 6)

    ■ As the believer opens up his heart enough for the Holy Spirit to fill him, he also opens up his heart to the free outward flow of Spirit-led expressions of joy and praises to God.

2. "Prayer tongues" for personal prayer and spiritual worship (Romans 8:26-27, 1 Corinthians 14:2, 15, 17)

    ■ The verbal expression of the human spirit of the Spirit-Baptized believer.

    ■ Aided or facilitated by the Holy Spirit.

    ■ Originate from the Holy Spirit dwelling with our human spirit.

    ■ Do not originate directly from the human mind or will—direct mind control is bypassed. Tongues of any kind (if genuine) can be quenched or withheld, but not really controlled. Like a light switch, they are either on or off.

    ■ Require our cooperation, a certain measure of surrender of the will, a willingness to be used.

    ■ Express human yearnings, desires, emotions, or deep-seated needs; possibly also spiritual realities (Romans 8:26-28).

    ■ Help us to pray according to God's will (Romans 8:26-28).

    ■ Edifies (builds up, strengthens) the human spirit (1 Cor. 14:4).

    ■ Not understood by the speaker (1 Cor. 14:14).

3. A sign to unbelievers that God is present and at work (Acts 2:6-13, 15; 1 Cor. 14:22).

4. A sign to the congregation that an interpretation (equivalent to prophecy) is forthcoming (1 Cor. 14:13, 27).

Appendix 6.   Word of Knowledge or Word of Wisdom?

I believe that in Acts 21 we have a clear example of the difference between a word of knowledge and a word of wisdom.

Full Gospel scholars, at least the "older" ones I have read, agree that these gifts are not knowledge itself or wisdom itself, as if those faculties were suddenly endowed bodily by the Holy Spirit, but a single "word" of knowledge or wisdom. In other words, the Spirit may enlighten a gifted believer with a certain pertinent fact or a timely item of wisdom on which to base a present decision.

Agabus, according to Acts 11:28, was one of several prophets who came to Antioch from Jerusalem. At that time, he "signified by the Spirit that there should be great dearth throughout all the world," *i.e.*, a famine. Armed with this information, the Antioch believers began a relief fund for the church in Judea. Clearly, Agabus' message was a word of knowledge. The Spirit told the church what would happen (knowledge) but not what to do about it (wisdom).

Later (Acts 21:10 ff.), Agabus met Paul in Caesarea. Binding his own hands with Paul's belt, he declared, "Thus saith the Holy Ghost, 'So shall the Jews at Jerusalem bind the man that owneth this girdle, and shall deliver him into the hands of the Gentiles.'" The other believers there took this message to be a word of wisdom (what to do) warning Paul not to return to Jerusalem.

Paul, however, took the message to be a word of knowledge (what would happen), insisting that he was "ready not to be bound only, but also to die at Jerusalem for the name of the Lord Jesus."

Obviously, believers need to learn the difference.

Appendix 7.   Brain Altered While Speaking in Tongues

Scientists at the University of Pennsylvania used brain scans to demonstrate altered brain activity while speaking in tongues, as described in a recent article in the science journal Psychiatry Research. According to a report by Benedict Carey (NY Times), neuroimages of five women during the act of speaking in tongues showed that the frontal lobes, associated with thinking and conscious control, as well as the language centers of the brain, were relatively inactive while speaking in tongues. In contrast, the women demonstrated increased activity while singing a Gospel song.

"The regions that are involved in maintaining self-consciousness were active: The women were not in a blind trance. It was unclear which region of their brain was driving their behavior," writes Carey.

The brain images are also in stark contrast to spiritual meditation, which rather stimulates the frontal lobes.

"The amazing thing was how the images supported people's interpretation of what was happening," said Dr. Andrew Newberg, the lead author. "The way they describe it, and what they believe, is that God is talking through them."

One of the researchers, Donna Morgan, is a Christian who speaks in tongues.

This research supports my own study and perception. In an article I published in *Paraclete* journal in 1992, I wrote:

> . . . Raymond T. Brock notes that the corpus collosum functions to provide communication between the hemispheres of the brain; or it can rather inhibit communication in order to make information more selective. He suggests that in verbal manifestations of the Spirit, the information can be made to bypass the cerebral cortex, which provides for direct control, and use only selected portions of the brain to operate the speech organs.

> . . . . The Holy Spirit does not at any time take control of a person. Paul makes it clear that the prophetic spirit of a prophet remains under his control (1 Corinthians 14:27-33) and that it is possible to "quench the Spirit" (I Thessalonians

5:19). It is in fact necessary for the gifted person to lend himself to the Spirit, yielding his control, his free will which the Spirit will not violate, to the use of the Spirit.

In order that a person speak God's message and not his own, then, it is necessary for the message to flow from within his true inner self, the subconscious, bypassing his direct control. The message must then emerge into the conscious realm, where it is pronounced by his organs of speech. The speaker remains perfectly aware of his actions and hears the message. The message is in the speaker's natural voice and is shaped by his speech patterns and orientation. It is, in fact, filtered through his conscious mind, though he has for the time being voluntarily relinquished control.[*]

Of course, some detractors of *glossolalia* will suggest that the conscious control of tongues comes from the devil. One might in turn ask them, "Where did the tongues in Acts 2:4 come from?"

Sources

Benedict Carey "A Neuroscientific Look at Speaking in Tongues," New York Times, November 7, 2006.

"The Measurement of Regional Cerebral Blood Flow During Glossolalia: A Preliminary SPECT Study" by Andrew B. Newberg, Nancy A. Wintering, Donna Morgan, and Mark R. Waldman.

---

[*] Paul Hughes, "The Holy Spirit and the Human Mind," *Paraclete* 26 (Spring 1992):17-22.

Appendix 8.   The True Spiritual Leader...

What I Have Learned about Spiritual Leadership

The spiritual leader:

- Is loathe to claim his authority.

- Is characterized by remarkable humility.

- Considers himself nothing, the Lord everything.

- Does not appoint himself everyone else's advisor, as if he knew all the answers, and others need to seek his approval.

- Can wait on the lord indefinitely, and will not be hurried by other agendas.

- Bases all his decisions on the lord's will.

- Never strives to accomplish god's work in his own strength.

- Does not trust in his own abilities.

- Does not question God.

- Is as content with obscurity as with visibility.

- Eschews personal honors and acclaim.

- Cares nothing for recognition or credit.

- Naturally mentors others, raises up spiritual leaders in kind.

- Feels no need to defend himself against criticism.

- Is willing to be misunderstood.

- Finds joy not in being successful, but in being faithful.

Appendix 9.   The Intercessor's Prayer

Lord, as I have felt called to be an intercessor for my church, its leadership, my community, for the salvation of souls, and any other need . . . .

Let me fulfill my calling as an intercessor, standing in the gap between the work of God and the works of Satan; casting down human reasoning; storming the gates of hell to pull down his strongholds; binding and defeating Satan in the lives of those whom he has oppressed . . . .

Teach me to pray, as James says, righteously, effectively, and fervently; putting this spiritual work first; willingly expending my time and energy to completely and in good conscience fulfill my calling; keeping my mind and body pure in order to be a holy vessel, fit for his service . . . .

Being always aware that I am not the spiritual authority over my pastor or my church, but am responsible to both. I am neither the pastor's head, to rule over him, nor the pastor's hands, to do his work, but an extra set of spiritual eyes and ears to help him see the Lord's vision, and hear the Lord's message to his Church; and an extra pair of lips to bring the needs of the Church before God's throne . . . .

Let me not become puffed up because of the abundance of the revelation working in me. Let me remain humble in your sight, because I know that it is with humility in the flesh, but boldness in the Spirit, that I must approach your throne, in order to hear your message and receive the answer.

Lord, I am your servant. Amen.

Select Index

Songs Written and Recorded by the Author

Contact the author for availability information

CD: Look Again (2003)

Look Again
Abide in the Vine (John 15:1-7)
Hebrews 12:12 ("Lift Up the Hands That Hang Down")
Guide My Steps, O Lord
Why Not Be Happy?
I Come to Light the World (John 12:44-49)
Yet I'll Trust in Him (Bach/Gounod, Job 13:15)
When All Your Dreams Are Gone
Surely Goodness (Psalm 23)

CD: Sow in Tears, Reap in Joy (2006)

When Life Goes Awry
Let Not Your Heart Be Troubled (John 14:1-3, 27)
I Was Lost and Alone (When You Came)
We Saw Him Die (Vittorio Monti, Czardas)
Gimme Gimme Gimme
Just Like Chasing a Leaf
My Life Was Empty (The Swan by Camille Saint-Saëns)
If Any My Serve Me (John 12:26)
Wherever You Go (He's There)
They That Sow in Tears (Shall Reap in Joy) (Ps 126:5-6, Mt 11:29, Gal 6:9)
So Send I You (John 20:21)

www.ingramcontent.com/pod-product-compliance
Lightning Source LLC
Chambersburg PA
CBHW032059080426
42733CB00006B/344